KT-116-622

WHO PROFITS?

Richard Adams

A LION PAPERBACK

Oxford · Batavia · Sydney

Text copyright © 1989 Richard Adams
This edition © 1989 Lion Publishing

Published by
Lion Publishing plc
Sandy Lane West, Littlemore, Oxford, England
ISBN 0 7459 1606 6
Lion Publishing Corporation
1705 Hubbard Avenue, Batavia, Illinois 60510, USA
ISBN 0 7459 1606 6
Albatross Books Pty Ltd
PO Box 320, Sutherland, NSW 2232, Australia
ISBN 0 7324 156 9

All rights reserved

British Library Cataloguing in Publication data
Adams, Richard
  Who profits?
  1. Developed countries. Economic relations with developing countries
  2. Developing countries.
  Economic relations with developed countries I. Title
  337'.09172'2
  ISBN 0 7459 1606 6

Printed and bound in Great Britain by Cox & Wyman Ltd, Reading

Contents

Introduction

This is not a book about a bunch of rabbits who set up a mail-order business. A couple of years ago, when I and my colleagues at Traidcraft were looking ahead to the company's tenth anniversary, we had the idea of asking a recognized author to chronicle the events and ideas that brought the company into being. I think that we all secretly fancied doing the job ourselves, but being up to the eyes in running an innovative, multi-million pound business gave little scope for considered reflection. In the event it became possible for me to spend the necessary months in front of a word processor; so, like a lot else in the development of Traidcraft, this book is a do-it-yourself job.

I hope that the momentum of events carries you over the many rough patches that will exclude the book from the ranks of the world's great literature. All the stylistic and factual errors are my own, although I would like to thank the many people who have pointed out the more obvious ones before they reached the printed page, and in particular Tim McClure, Geoff Howard, Jan Simmonds, Brian Hutchins, Graham Young, Ray Skinner, Joan Waterhouse and Chris Rowland. My wife Chris has combined a sharp eye with constructive support and has exercised a moderating influence, as indeed she has done on many occasions in the past years.

The biography of a company is in many ways similar to that

of a person. I have found myself leaving out vast chunks of material that were the everyday stuff of existence and selected only happenings that seem to have played a formative role. The choice is entirely mine and I have been unashamedly subjective. This book, therefore, in no way represents the view of Traidcraft plc about itself, and inevitably what I have chosen to relate leaves much that is important to one side.

Although many people are mentioned in the text, there are many who made major contributions to Traidcraft who are not. The fact that only a dozen members of Traidcraft staff, out of a possible two hundred past and present, are identified by name is not to protect the innocent but to avoid confusing the reader. Traidcraft started as a collaborative venture and developed on that basis, so the few staff, board members, reps and partners from producing groups overseas who are mentioned stand for all.

What I have tried to do is follow the way in which an idea came to be put into practice. As a result the ideas, the people and the day-to-day aspects of running a business are intertwined. We have never laid claim to much original thinking within Traidcraft, but we do stitch ideas together and then make them work. As a result the story starts well before Traidcraft was born and will continue not only in the work of Traidcraft staff, suppliers and customers but in other initiatives that put people before profit. We all want to change the world, to make it a better place. This book tries to show how a group of people set about bringing love and justice into international trade as their contribution.

1

Fruit and Jute

The dogs ate asparagus, and the people enjoyed many of the world's most exotic fruits and vegetables. Was this paradise? Not exactly! But for the two families living over Turner's Stores in Sudbury Hill, these luxuries provided some compensation for working eighteen hours a day, seven days a week.

It was here, in the kitchen of a flat above a large greengrocer's shop in north-west London, that some of the most exotic meals in Britain were prepared during 1973. Who noticed if most of the ingredients were slightly past their best? Who worried if occasionally the aroma of fifteen tonnes of disintegrating green peppers escaped from the downstairs cold store? This was the hub of a venture bringing the products of the tropics to the people of Britain: capsicums for Clapham, mouli for Muswell Hill and bhindi for Birmingham. This was the beginning of Traidcraft.

All my working life since university has been spent in business of one form or another. In the last fifteen years I have been devoted to starting and running companies that are seeking an alternative approach to trade. To me this means taking a radical position as I apply Christian perspectives to both strategy and management. The challenges have increased as the companies have grown, so even as managing director of a multi-million pound public company I have still found my work a mixture of immense excitement and deep uncertainty.

In 1968 I was about to begin training for the ordained ministry in the Church of England. Then the discomfort began. Gradually I realized that I was not seeing the church as the great and glorious structure that it seemed to some but more as an enduring temporary hut at the edge of a building site. I was seeing it as a depot for tools and resources — a place to shelter from rough weather, discuss how the job was to be done and debate the architect's plans. I noticed that, for some, it seemed to be a place to sign on and sign off. But the doubt grew: what was the church doing to tackle the *real* work of the world. What became important for me then, and remains so now, was action to bring justice into a world where billions suffered needlessly.

So, on leaving college, I apologized to the bishop and, with a diploma in theology under one arm and degree in social theory under the other, set off into the world of what I thought was real work. The year was 1968 and it was a good time to think about the nature of work, its ethics and its purpose. The intellectual climate was stimulating: being radical was not only popular, it was almost obligatory. Most important, however, there was plenty of work around: with unemployment at only 3 per cent, I had the luxury of choice.

Then, even more so than now, those who were fundamentally ill at ease with the injustices of the world first turned to the caring professions, but it was here that my sociology background intervened. I knew that the care-givers tried to solve problems, but who made the mess in the first place? The earliest civilizations controlled the force of rivers by forcing thousands of workers to build impressive dams. Their modern counterparts, the industrial/technical/military combines of West and East, were still controlling the flow of resources and capital. It was those in power who determined the life opportunities of thousands of millions. I did not think I had the temperament for a career in politics and there were indications that I might not get on too well in the armed forces. As an NCO in the school cadet force I had been court-martialled for turning a training camp exercise in the Welsh hills into a replica of the battle of Rorke's Drift, inspired by the film *Zulu* that was on general release at the time.

All that was left was business. I was already half convinced, and have become more so since, that it is our commercial structures, which shape our attitude to wealth, possessions, and the values we attach to them, that are the keys to real influence in present Western society.

The link between running a greengrocer's shop and changing the world may not be obvious at first sight. It began with an essay competition for the Food and Agriculture Organization of the UN. *What is the most effective way to bring prosperity to the agricultural communities of less developed nations? (10,000 words max.)* I discussed this question with Mike Schluter, an economist friend at college, and it soon became clear to us that the large-scale production of artificial fertilizers would be the answer. It was not, and our essay did not win the prize. What did happen was that through the research we undertook we began to learn about the needs of the rural poor in the Third World. Mike was fired with a similar enthusiasm for change and justice, and so we began to discuss more realistic plans for how we might be most effective.

We needed experience and specific skills. After a year in East Africa, Mike began a PhD at Cornell University in the United States. His topic was agricultural economics, specializing in the difficulties faced by the small farmers in Gujarat, India. I got a job as Assistant Industrial Development Officer with the North East Development Council in Newcastle-upon-Tyne. Mike was to become the specialist in rural development economics, and I was to acquire practical business skills. At first we retained enthusiasm for our fertilizer plant, but ideas came and went with our correspondence. After two years I moved on to become a fully-fledged industrial officer for East Lothian County Council in Scotland. The years I spent finding out what mattered to firms who wanted to expand would, we hoped, come in useful later. At the same time Mike went to India for a year and spent several months in the villages of Surat District. In 1972, using two years' accumulated leave, I spent six weeks with him there.

Our plans were taking shape. Small farmers usually only planted subsistence crops that they and their families could store for some time and eat as they needed them. Some other

11

types of produce could be counted as cash crops, because the farmers could sell them for a good price in the local markets. Too often, however, there would be a glut of these crops and then the price would go right down. French beans that normally sold for 5p a kilo would fetch just 1p. There was no easy way to store the beans in a hot climate, and so the farmers' work would be virtually wasted.

But what if there was some way to ensure that the farmers could guarantee a better price? In London's Covent Garden wholesale market, 6,000 miles away, the price of french beans never went below 70p a kilo, and averaged about twenty times as much as the Indian wholesale price. Jumbo jets had just been introduced, international travel was expanding and air-freight prices were low. Put all the pieces together, we argued, and the affluent in Britain would willingly be paying good money to the small farmers in India and everyone would be happy. This seemed a much better bet than huge industrial fertilizer plants, which the World Bank was now funding anyway following the early successes of the Green Revolution. More important, we could implement the scheme ourselves and did not have to work our way into the higher levels of a big commercial company. I have frequently wondered since how many naive enthusiasts have taken the established career route and been transformed into sensible and successful industrialists.

That first visit to India was also my first experience of a developing country. Everything was new and clamoured for attention, from the roadside vultures to the thousands of prisoners crowded behind barbed wire following the war with Pakistan a few months earlier. As I left the plane in Bombay I thought that the engines were still running, blasting their hot exhaust over the disembarkation steps. I later discovered that it was the cool night breeze from the Arabian Sea. Dozens of visits later I am still affected by that cocktail of heat, smell and noise. Many people find that culture shock sharpens their awareness. It certainly did for me that first time.

It took several weeks and the tranquillity of Indian village life for me to begin to come to terms with this instinctive revulsion against poverty, disease and tawdriness. I later learnt that the peace of the villages was in some ways an illusion. Only too often the village was a dead end, without facilities, without work, and with only too many obligations to the landlord and the moneylender. But it was as I walked from village to village with Mike, accompanying him on his survey of crops grown by small farmers, that another type of culture shock began to take hold.

We had stopped in the evening at the village shop, which was really more like a large booth tacked onto a small mud-brick hut. The family was gathered in the hut doorway. It comprised about ten people, some very young, one very old. 'This is my father,' the English-speaking shopkeeper told us. 'He is dying, you know.' He translated into Gujarati for the rest of the family. They all smiled broadly and nodded; some of them touched the old man encouragingly, and he gave a toothless smile himself. There was no fear, embarrassment or even pity. Such a calm and positive acceptance of death absorbed it into life itself. I began to realize how deep were the roots that could nourish this attitude and that people with few possessions can still have much to give.

But these positive experiences only fully emerge in moments of subsequent reflection. My overwhelming emotion when faced with much of daily life in the Third World, both then and now, is anger. Why the suffering, the hope cut off, the injustice and the barriers to human and spiritual growth that the Western traveller sees confronting those in the developing world? We have our own barriers to growth, of course, but not these: not ones that can be removed with a fraction of the resources that we squander on our entertainment, extra comfort or peace of mind.

In 1936, with the country still suffering the effects of the depression, King Edward VIII had caused a scandal by saying of the position of the unemployed in South Wales that 'something must be done'. The very mildness of the phrase seemed all the more threatening by its assumption that ordinary, decent people should naturally not tolerate injustice. Those of us who are angry at injustice, and that probably means most people, need to think carefully about our feelings. Our sense of outrage is made up of the clear, bright anger that no human being ought to suffer from injustice. But also we are angry at others who have caused the problem and who perpetuate it: 'they' should not have acted as they did or allowed the problem to continue. And underlying all this we are angry with ourselves and ashamed of our security and prosperity. We need to dig down to expose this anger about ourselves, because if it lies buried it will rot inside us and secretly infect our best intentions. Open it up to the light and it can harden into a place to stand, a base for action.

So while Mike was completing his doctorate in America I began writing to commercial estate agents in the suburbs of west London, asking about greengrocer's shops. We needed experience in the trade and we needed a base that had a cold store near Heathrow and Gatwick. Turner's Stores was ideal: a thriving business with its own big insulated store to keep produce at five degrees Celsius, situated in an ethnically-mixed area. We also had the chance to keep on a young and enthusiastic manager whose family had been in the greengrocery trade for generations. Now we had to take the plunge.

From a personal point of view it was not the easiest time to launch into something new. My wife Chris and I had met at university and married soon after. Our first child was born in Edinburgh not long after I returned from my first visit to India. Within days we were told that he had a serious heart problem. Weeks of increasing concern culminated in Chris accompanying the child in an incubator on a flight to London and Great Ormond Street Hospital. I joined her before the operation. It was to involve a procedure that was just being developed, and we were told that Edmund had a very slim chance of surviving.

Surgery took place late at night and was not successful. There is no easy way of dealing with that sort of loss. Logically we knew that for most people suffering and pain are curiously part of the trade-off against joy and fulfilment. But when a personal tragedy strikes, then the faith that is unable to provide an explanation but still says that, somehow, all will be well, is stretched to the limit. Nevertheless, the work involved in starting Agrofax Labour Intensive Products Ltd, as the new business was called, helped cover up the sense of emptiness and waste that we both felt.

The majority of small business start-ups are under-funded, and ours was no exception. We needed about £12,000 to start the company and wondered where it was to come from. I handed in my notice to the county council, we sold our house in Scotland and, with that money and what we could raise from the bank against insurance policies, managed to go halves with Mike on the opening capital. He still had several months' work to complete on his doctorate and we realized that another person would need to be involved. Then I heard that another college friend of ours, Tim McClure, who had been an Anglican curate for three years in Huddersfield, would soon be on the lookout for a new position. He struck me as the ideal person to join the partnership, not least because he knew that courgettes were a type of vegetable rather than a Chuck Berry song title. I gave him a ring.

'How would you like to be a greengrocer in London?' I asked. 'So long as you don't mind my eating the stock it sounds great,' he replied. He was clearly able to switch from one type of pastoral ministry to another, lured as he was by the vision of artichokes in butter and fresh mangoes.

So there we were: Tim with his wife Barbie and their three-year-old son Matthew; Chris and I; and Spike and Minnie, the dogs with the growing taste for asparagus spears. We were good friends, which was especially fortunate as we all shared a small, two-bedroom flat over the shop.

A typical day started at 5 a.m. when we drove the lorry to Brentford wholesale market. After buying stock for the shop we returned to unload and watch in awe as Alan 'Groper' Brookes, the shop manager we had inherited, produced pyramids of fruit in a matter of minutes for our display. We had the best 'flash' on the entire length of the Greenford Road. It was just the thing to draw in the punters. Groper was proud of his skills. His only regret was that handling so much fruit and vegetables had one big drawback: 'My hands get so rough,' he confided to Tim and I, 'that I'm always snagging my girlfriend's tights.'

There was a lot to learn about the greengrocery trade. Our education was further broadened as we discovered the varying shades of grey that colour its day-to-day practices. If we were lucky we would be faced with a straightforward moral decision: we were quite clear that keeping a thumb on the scale when weighing goods was definitely out. More often, though, we had to decide was what level of compromise to adopt. We were shown how to freshen up lettuces and cabbages, how to turn small old potatoes into tasty new ones with the aid of the bath and a bag of peat, and how to 'improve' yellowing sprouts. This could be done in two stages. First you stripped off one layer of outer leaves and trimmed the bottom. Trimmed sprouts were worth an extra 4p a pound. A more cost-effective operation, however, was to remove several sets of outer leaves so that the sprouts were reduced to a third of their original size. These kernels could now be called 'button sprouts' and were worth another 10p a pound. We certainly had no qualms about going round our salad displays with the watering can before we opened in the morning. 'There you are, dear, lovely and fresh. Look, it's still got the dew on it!' The extra dousing kept the produce fresh, we did not charge for it and the customers were happy to collude in the fiction.

Some tricks of the trade seemed sensible and legitimate, but others were highly dubious, and we puzzled Groper with our refusal to adopt some of his techniques.

Our own contributions to greengrocers' lore were in the fields of art and sport. Using misshapen tomatoes, mushrooms, radishes and other stock we fashioned edible figures that sat on the counter near the cash register. In slack moments we also perfected the art of hurling an over-ripe tomato between us down the length of the shop. The real skill was in catching a tomato whole rather than as a puré. On top of all this our customers effortlessly provided enough distinctive characters to cast a dozen television series.

About 6.30 p.m. we would push up the blind, roll down the shutter and head for our elaborate dinner upstairs. After an excellent meal we would turn to the other side of the business. Twice a week a shipment of exotic fruit and vegetables would arrive at Heathrow or Gatwick. Sometimes we would get a few hours' notice of a delivery; other times sometimes our air-freight agent would ring to say that three tons of produce had arrived and needed rapid clearance. We would bump-start whichever of our two clapped-out lorries was roadworthy and drive to the airport. If we were lucky we could be loaded within two hours; occasionally it would take half a day.

Having collected a shipment we had to sell it. Phone calls around our commission agents in the London markets determined how much they thought they could take and we delivered the following night. We loaded up the lorry again and began the trek: Western International at Hounslow, Covent Garden, Borough in Southwark and Spitalfields. The London fruit and vegetable markets were peopled by characters who appeared to have stepped straight out of the pages of Dickens. We always used to look forward to meeting Charlie, the night porter at E.C. Dean in Covent Garden. Charlie knew about the hidden properties of fruits and vegetables, especially asparagus. This particular vegetable, he claimed, had amazing descaling properties in the waterworks. You could tell that its medicinal properties were having the right effect, he said, 'because it came up at yer'. We quickly found out what he meant once our first Kenyan shipment of the stuff arrived and we had the chance to consume some of the rejects and allow nature to take its course.

As time went on and shipments increased we began delivering to Leicester and Birmingham markets to serve the large immigrant communities there. The main difficulty was getting to these centres. One night Tim and I were driving a four-ton shipment up the M1 in our two-ton lorry when we were stopped by the police. As our starter motor had gone we did not dare turn off the engine. The handbrake did not work either, so I had to keep my foot on both accelerator and brake as Tim convinced them that we really did have a load of mangoes on board as we had claimed. 'Get this thing off the road, quick!' was their parting comment.

The regular traders at the markets quickly identified us as newcomers to the business. Not only was it obvious that we were 'college boys'; occasionally the staggering fact that Tim was also an ordained clergyman would emerge. Not that the visible face of religion was entirely absent from the markets. Nuns could often be seen bargaining for cheap produce for their old people's homes. Once we saw two clergy attired in cassocks and collars being hailed by a chorus of wolf-whistles from the porters. Experiences such as the latter encouraged us to keep a low profile.

At the same time as we were getting our act together to help the Third World, a major attempt at self-help on the part of the poorer nations was also being organized. Within months of our setting up in business, OPEC decided to show some muscle and raise oil prices. The resulting crisis hit the industrialized world in general and Agrofax Labour Intensive Products in particular. All forms of oil products, including aviation fuel, underwent massive price rises. Very cheap freight rates became a thing of the past. We began to wonder where Agrofax might be going. It was at this time, in mid 1974, that I got a call from Ian Prior, an old college acquaintance who was working with an evangelical relief and development agency called TEAR Fund.

'Richard, would you be interested in meeting Peter McNee? He's a New Zealand Baptist missionary who works in Bangladesh.' I knew Ian quite well so I began to formulate an impolite refusal. He went on undaunted: 'He's here on behalf of a co-operative selling jute handicrafts and you're the only person I could think of who's importing anything from overseas.'

Later that week Peter arrived at the shop with a large brown suitcase. When he lifted the lid it appeared to be full of bits of string, which he called 'sikas' and which turned out to be hanging baskets. As he unpacked them he told us about the background of a group called the Jute Works. It was a training and marketing co-operative that had just been set up by some of the church and development agencies in Dhaka. Hundreds of thousands of women had been widowed in the fighting against Pakistan in 1971, and their situation had been made worse by a cyclone and flooding in subsequent years. They desperately needed some means to earn an income, and doing macramé work in jute was a traditional skill that offered some possibilities. Could we help by buying some of the products? They were urgently needing orders now that the first groups were trained and had already sold all they could in the local market.

The decision seemed to make itself. Yes, we would order a

range of the sikas, baskets, bags and mats. We ordered about £1000 worth altogether, to be air-freighted from Dhaka within three months. We had no idea of how we were going to sell them but that shiny, golden jute with the intricate braiding looked so attractive that we felt we would be able to manage it when the time came. Peter looked around the shop on his way out. 'I feel quite at home here,' he said, 'It's just like the market in Chandpur, except that your potatoes are cheaper.' The next time I met Peter was, in fact, on the ferry jetty at Chandpur in southern Bangladesh. He told me then, 'I thought you were mad, a greengrocer buying jute, but I certainly was not going to complain. I should know by now that God's world is full of surprises.'

I've often wondered why we plunged into trading in jute handicrafts so readily. Perhaps it was as a result of my earlier visit to rural India when I had noticed that there was often some form of craft work being done in the house, around the village, or even out in the fields. Craft work rarely required sophisticated equipment and could be started or left at any time. This approach was ideal for agricultural communities who have periods of intense activity around sowing and harvest but a slower pace of life at other times. Crafts normally used local raw materials such as palm leaf, sisal, clay, reeds, bamboo, cane and jute. The skills were often handed down within the family and reflected a long tradition. Often the decoration would also reflect the culture of the area and all this, together with the fact that children could join in on the simpler tasks, made craft work a binding force within the family and the community. It was not necessary to travel to a town, to have electricity or to buy expensive equipment.

Not least craft work provided a very useful income. Handicrafts earned real money, just like the cash crop that was often a great risk for a farmer to grow, but had several advantages: they were not perishable, they could be stored or transported easily and often were quite valuable. In most cases the value of the craft was in the labour and skill that had gone into making it, not in the raw material. However, the local market for them was quickly satisfied. It was clear that an export market would fetch better prices for the craft workers.

Some of this thinking must have been underlying our decision to buy our first half ton of handicrafts. In retrospect it did seem to be a logical extension of the vegetable business, although at the time it was far more impulsive. A number of other changes were also taking place. Tim had successfully applied for a job as chaplain at Manchester Polytechnic and would be taking up the position in the autumn. Mike Schluter had been investigating ways of sun-drying vegetables as they were harvested and was considering going to Kenya to work, particularly as we felt that the greengrocery business was struggling to support us all directly.

Our own family circumstances had changed as well. At the end of April Chris had given birth to Zoë at the newly-opened Northwick Park Hospital. Naturally we were concerned, but we were relieved to discover that our second baby was fine. Barbie and Tim had also had a second baby a few months earlier, and our shared two-bedroom flat had become extremely cosy for the three children, four adults and two dogs. In the summer of 1974 we escaped for a week's break at a friend's cottage in rural Northumberland, and a different piece of the jigsaw emerged.

Ray Skinner was another old friend from college who had declined more adventurous options and gone into the Anglican ministry! He was then a curate in Elswick, an inner-city parish in Newcastle-upon-Tyne. Ray and his wife Hilary were living in a large terrace house that had a two-room basement. It had become a store for the many cannibalized spare parts Ray needed to keep his low-cost transport running. One day, as we struggled with the indoor sprinkler system that Ray optimistically refered to as plumbing, he asked, 'Why don't you start a mail-order business for these handicrafts at Victoria Street? I could put together some shelves and Hilary could do the packing.' 'I'll think about it, Ray,' I said, 'Newcastle's quite a long way from London, you know.'

In fact mail-order did seem a good idea. We thought that we would be able to put together a mailing list of a couple of hundred people and rely on word-of-mouth to some extent. We had many friends employed in the church and their individual churches had congregations who might be interested in the story behind the handicrafts and in the goods themselves. Newcastle seemed remote, but I knew from working there for two years how good the business facilities were if we ever needed to expand. Property was a lot cheaper than in London, and for the same wages a much higher material standard of living was available. All in all it was a serious possibility, so on our return to Sudbury Hill I began a correspondence with Ray about how we might proceed.

Late summer and early autumn saw the widest range of English fruits available sitting in the shop alongside the passion fruit, mangoes and pineapples that we had imported ourselves. Most of our fruit and vegetables were coming from Kenya, and most of those from estates rather than small farms. There was still a lot of work to do in helping the small growers to supply produce for export, usually through a co-operative. Occasionally we got produce from Uganda, a country increasingly in turmoil under General Amin's government. In one unexpected shipment we received fifteen tonnes of root ginger. As this amount was probably enough to supply all of Britain for a week we ended up selling it for only a few pence a pound. The Ugandans were desperate for any income from abroad and even this tiny contribution was welcome.

In mid-October our agents phoned to say that a shipment of handicrafts had arrived at Heathrow on flight TG996 from Dhaka. We collected it, together with a consignment of french beans and courgettes from Nairobi, and stacked it next to the cold store. I phoned Ray and asked him if his basement was ready. 'It looks as if we will be able to get something out before Christmas,' I said. 'As soon as we've checked it I'll put a leaflet together to send round to all our contacts.'

That first promotional sheet listed eleven items. As it turned out, we had decided to start the mail-order business from Turner's Stores. Hilary was expecting a baby in November and had a few reservations about her combined role as first-time parent and packer-in-chief. However, the leaflet did make the following announcement.

21

> We hope soon to have in stock the full range of products amounting to some fifty items and to issue an illustrated catalogue early in 1975.

It showed that I had decided to take the craft business more seriously. Indeed, I had placed a second order with a more extensive range from the Jute Works and I planned that the 'illustrated catalogue' would be serviced from Newcastle. Three months seemed to be enough for Hilary to get the hang of being a mother. But again, providence intervened, once more in the form of a phone call from Ian Prior of TEAR Fund.

'Did you get anywhere with that order for jute that you placed after Peter McNee's visit?' he queried. 'Actually, Ian,' I said, 'It's just arrived and we are working out ways to sell it right now.' 'Oh, that's interesting,' he said. 'I wonder if you would like to come down to our office and talk to George about a relief flight we're planning. I've told him you might be able to help.'

The following day I was talking to George Hoffman, the director of TEAR Fund, in his office at Teddington. George had been an assistant editor of the Christian magazine *Crusade* when it had launched an appeal for disaster relief in 1968, in conjunction with the Evangelical Alliance. The excellent response gave birth to TEAR Fund and it had been George's rapidly-growing baby since then. George was telling me about the needs of Bangladesh, a place he had recently visited. 'They just have nothing there: no food in the shops and no drugs or medicines, so we are considering chartering a cargo plane, filling it with blankets, powdered milk and basic medical supplies and getting it to fly out straight away.'

I told him what I knew about air-freight and cargo chartering, which was not very much. 'Well, it's the return leg where we thought you might be able to help. We have to pay about $20,000 for the flight and the plane is coming back empty. Ian tells me that you've had experience of buying handicrafts. Do you think you could go out ahead of the relief flight and get enough together from these community groups to make a good cargo for the return?'

I managed to control my surprise and asked a practical

question about who was going to pay. George assured me that TEAR Fund would cover all expenses and asked me how much a plane-load of handicrafts would cost. I made a guess: '£10,000.' 'There's only one problem,' said George. 'We have the plane booked for two weeks' time, so you'll have to hurry.' It was only after I had left that I realized I had not asked what TEAR Fund was going to do with the handicrafts once they arrived.

I think that Chris only believed what I told her the following day when a cheque for £10,000 payable to R. Adams arrived in the post. There was a rush to get visas, inoculations and foreign currency and to book a flight. We postponed sending out our mail-order leaflet. Tim and family had by now moved to Manchester and Chris would be fully occupied keeping an eye on the shop and the importing business. Several cable messages were sent to Bangladesh, but there were no replies, so I had to hope that someone would know about my visit before I got there. Looking back I do not think that I had any qualms about flying to an unknown city in a country wracked with violence and the desperation of poverty to buy a plane-load of handicrafts on the spot. Being a greengrocer must have prepared me for anything. On 12 November I boarded the British Airways flight to Dhaka with a suitcase full of toilet rolls and Smarties, assured by George that they were much sought-after commodities in the expatriate community.

2

Crafts to Newcastle

There did not seem to be anywhere to land. As the VC10 circled Dhaka, all that I could see in the fading light was water and what appeared to be a large island in the shape of a monkey holding chopsticks. Water channels seemed to weave everywhere. This impression was reinforced later when I visited the villages, many of which were isolated by the rising rivers for weeks at a time during the monsoon season. 'Flat and wet' is how one encyclopaedia eloquently describes Bangladesh.

I had underestimated how difficult it was to communicate with Dhaka. Although a cable saying I was coming had been sent a week earlier to HEED, TEAR Fund's partners in Bangladesh, it did not arrive for a further three days. No one was there to meet me so I waited only a few minutes in the dark outside the small airport building that was pitted with bullet and shrapnel marks from the recent violence. I had heard that a curfew was operating for part of the night so, rather than wait longer, I hired one of the motorized rickshaws known as baby-taxis. By this means I arrived at the address in the Dhanmandi district of Dhaka that I had been given and was dropped off outside a barred gate. I eventually persuaded the gate man or *chokidar* to let me in and restrain his apparently very hungry dog.

I knocked smartly on the house door, but there was no reply. I knocked again. First the *chokidar* and then his dog joined me in my efforts. At last the door was opened by an extremely apprehensive lady. Hester Quirk, who had spent many years in the less comfortable parts of the world, had good reason to be worried. Dhaka was a city of violent desperation, and neighbouring houses had been broken into frequently. Earlier in the week the knifed body of a man had been found a few doors away. Hester was responsible for the eight young nurses who lived in the house; she felt vulnerable, and my arrival probably made things worse. Suitcases and boxes had to be removed from a large cupboard in order to improvise a bedroom for me. By the morning I had discovered that this little nook was also the centre of mosquito high-life. No matter what the heat or humidity, I learnt, a night spent hermetically sealed and sweating under a thick sheet is preferable to days of itching.

From then on my trip got better. My first call the next morning was to the Jute Works. Information about my visit had failed to reach the people there, but they recognized me as one of their overseas customers, even though my order had been a small one. I explained that I hoped to buy enough handicrafts to fill up a large cargo plane. Disbelief turned to amazement and then to jubilant enthusiasm. The Jute Works took on the atmosphere of Santa's Workshop, with eager helpers rushing to fill my sleigh! They would not have enough from their own stock; people would be sent to the village production centres and asked to send all that they could. Would I take seconds? Would I take palm leaf mats, crochet work and embroidery? Would I take bamboo furniture, cane baskets and sweeping brushes? Yes, I said, I would take almost anything that might sell in Britain provided that it did not come to more than fifteen tonnes and one hundred cubic metres or £10,000 altogether.

There were seven days before the plane was due from the UK with its cargo of blankets and powdered milk. Soon the storage space of the Jute Works was overflowing, and the garden of the house that served as the offices became an open-air warehouse. Whilst crafts were being assembled I took a ferry down one of the many branches of the Ganges/Jamuna to Chandpur to visit Peter McNee. Further down the delta, nearer the sea, people had been more badly affected by the cyclone and the tidal waves that had swept inland for many miles. Peter was still mainly concerned with the construction of housing to replace what had been lost. Could there really be a link between this devastated landscape and a greengrocer's shop in Sudbury Hill? What was going to happen to those bales of jute stored beside the potatoes in Turner's Stores and to the tonnes of products currently being assembled in Dhaka? I really did not have any idea, but, as I was to find out, other people thought that I did.

The Baptist Mission at Chandpur had become a natural focus for relief and rehabilitation work after the cyclone and flooding. One reason was that it had effective links with sources of help outside the locality. However, as the entire country had been depleted of resources, it was the mission's links beyond Bangladesh that were vital now. Obtaining safe water, food, clothing and housing had been the initial priorities; the second stage of rehabilitation was finding a way to make people who had lost everything self-reliant once again. Peter recognized that the handicrafts offered a reasonably quick way of generating some income. After training, an individual could be earning a very basic income within three months.

When I returned to Dhaka the following day the pile in front of the Jute Works seemed far too big to fit inside the aircraft that was due to arrive in five days. Most of the goods from the nearby villages had arrived, and I spent some time getting to know the other organizations that had contributed to the mound. I was told that 'relief' was Bangladesh's fastest-growing industry and that more than 150 different foreign agencies had offices established in Dhaka. The weight of the local bureaucracy was matched only by the lack of co-ordination between the development groups. It was not the field officers who were to blame: they usually had excellent working relationships with each other. The real difficulty, I realized later, was that each agency had to demonstrate to its own supporters that it was providing a particular package of development assistance. There were schemes to help children, the blind, lepers, co-operative workers, women, socialists, Catholics and Protestants. In theory most of the population would fall into one or more categories; in practice there was some overlap and many gaps, and I began to plan, from my vast experience of nearly five days, possible strategies for integrating the increasing help coming into a country that the American secretary of state Henry Kissinger had called 'a basket case'.

Fortunately there were so many practical things to do that I did not take this reforming crusade very far. I visited more villages and self-help groups. Bangladesh struck me as very different from India. In its former status as East Pakistan it had for twenty years been neglected by the government in West Pakistan. In early 1971 the Bengali people took up armed resistance against their repressive government. The Pakistani army was sent in to quell the uprising and terrible atrocies ensued over an eight-month period. An estimated three million people were killed and ten million flooded across the borders with India to escape. India intervened, fighting Pakistan on two fronts. After a fourteen-day campaign, in December 1971, Bangladesh became independent. The 93,000 soldiers from East Pakistan surrendered to the Indian Army, which in turn had to protect the soldiers from the people they had been attacking in the previous months.

The euphoria that accompanied the end of the war and the start of independence was short lived. The wealth of Bangladesh had been drained off under the period of colonial rule, and this process continued while it was under the domination of West Pakistan. The main industries had collapsed during the war. All the main bridges had been destroyed, and so had a lot of the rail network and half of the river transport systems. There was no food for the people. Major international programmes were needed to develop the skills of the people and to create rural employment and an industrial base for the country.

At this critical time in its development Bangladesh was the victim of massive government incompetence and corruption. Then, in the summer of 1974, came the worst floods in living memory, which inundated 40 per cent of the land. Hundreds began to die every day. Typhoid and cholera spread in the wake of the devastation and starvation was widespread.

Thousands of destitute people crowded the streets of Dhaka. Aid was pouring in, but it could barely cover short-term needs. The political situation was extremely volatile and so there was very little foreign investment. Occasionally I heard gunfire at night. I was told that I had run a serious risk travelling after dark. Within a short time, longer curfews were introduced.

Away from the city, however, these problems were less apparent. As I travelled around the villages near Dhaka that had formed jute handicraft cooperatives I got to know some of the people responsible for establishing them. Sister Mike (short for Michael Francis) had been working in East Pakistan for ten years. She was a nun from California and was now based in the Holy Cross Convent in Dhaka. In 1968 she had begun a systematic training programme for village women. They would come to Dhaka for an eight-week course bringing their own jute, needles and scissors. At the centre the women learned the basics of cooperative working and many of them returned home to start a local co-operative.

Jagaroni, the training centre, was run by Dolly and Patricia, both deaf mutes who had come from an oppressive family background. Traditionally any form of handicap is regarded as an embarrassment to the family, and as young girls they had both been shut away and neglected. When they moved to the training centre their families were asked to sign papers saying that in future they would not expect support from their daughters, as would normally be expected from an unmarried woman. Now both girls were earning their own living, and the mere fact of their independence provided inspiration and incentive for village women who had very low status themselves.

This programme was just one example of the link between income and emancipation that was to become such a key element in work for justice and liberation in the future. The domestic responsibilities of Bangladeshi women demanded hard, physical work that might last from 6 a.m. to 10 p.m. There were few of the conveniences that we take for granted, and social life was often restricted to the village or even the *bari* or home compound. In this setting a cooperative could have an amazing effect. It provided the opportunity for women to meet others, to travel, to organize and to save. Previously there was little opportunity for women to contribute to the income of the family or village. A cooperative enabled them to move up the scale; although they were still regarded as chattels they were also viewed as potential earners. Sometimes the savings of the cooperative could be used to provide a village well, a sewing machine or a piece of land. Growing economic strength earned the women respect, and education was no longer seen as a waste but as an investment, for a girl might become the secretary of the cooperative in time. Perhaps her marriage could be delayed to let her finish training or complete her studies. All this, however, only affected the few, only reached some hundreds of villages out of more than sixty thousand.

This pattern of development from simple beginnings is not only seen in Bangladesh but all over the world where people who have been on the margin have begun to acquire resources of their own. It is a pattern that can be applied to relations between the rich world and the poor world in general. We have become used to sharing our planet with people who are regarded as a sub-class and an embarrassment. The potential for them to prosper is there, but we in the industrialized world can now pull all the economic strings or have them pulled on our behalf. It is not in our immediate economic interest to help the poorest, so we give them a pittance out of our surplus. Even the biggest donor of aid in the world, Japan, only provides a third of a per cent of its gross national product as assistance. This pattern of aid is unlikely to change, so it becomes all the more important for us to tackle world poverty in another way. Our help must come not from what we have left over after we have provided for our needs or fancies but through the very process of providing for ourselves. Fair trade and directing our spending in a positive way is essential.

The relief flight was delayed by a couple of days, so I had a little extra time to learn about the needs of different groups, but eventually the converted Britannia turbo-prop airliner landed. The tail swung open and the work of unloading the supplies began. As I saw how much was coming out I began to wonder whether we had enough to fill the space after all. When we loaded the handicrafts the following morning my fears were confirmed: they filled just two-thirds of the volume and were well under the weight allowance. I agreed with the Jute Works that I would take all its reject work, which looked perfectly good to me, but even so there was still space. Eventually I toured Dhaka in a lorry, stopping at roadside stalls that sold cane and bamboo furniture to buy tables, chairs and bookcases. I did not know at the time that the bamboo furniture had an interesting feature: it could manufacture small piles of sawdust on a daily basis. This intriguing fact only emerged months later, when the beetles responsible became active in the houses all over Britain to which the bookcases had been dispersed.

At last the plane was full and I said goodbye to the many people I had come to know well in the ten days I had spent in Bangladesh. 'See you soon,' I told them with some confidence, for an idea about how to sell their products had been emerging in my mind as I talked with the different groups. Flying can often be boring, but travelling as a passenger on a freight plane certainly is not. We flew lower and slower than a jet and were accompanied by an overpowering smell of eucalyptus oil, the remains of the previous cargo. Crates of soft drinks were stacked against the door, where they rapidly froze, but there was plenty of room to stretch out and have a proper sleep under a pile of blankets. After about twenty-five hours we landed at Stansted. The handicrafts went into a warehouse, and I returned to Chris and Zoë at Turner's Stores wondering whether my ideas for a new type of trading business would work.

The next day I was able to put my delayed question to George Hoffman: What was TEAR Fund going to do with the shipment? 'I was hoping that you would have some ideas about that,' replied George. 'Why don't you put something together and we can talk about it next week?' I explained to George that storing eleven tonnes of bulky crafts in the bonded warehousing at Stansted was very expensive and that the goods needed clearing through customs. Did TEAR Fund have an agent or import registration details? Somewhat to my surprise it was suggested that Agrofax should take title to the goods, clear them and arrange for their storage. Meanwhile I would produce some suggestions on what to do with them then.

Tony, who lived in the flat next door, was a removal man, and we quickly had the shipment moved into a large furniture depository in Willesden. I have since wondered how many termites and bamboo beetles took the chance to jump ship at that stage. Before long the products were on the move again, this time into the space below the floorboards of a school gym in Newcastle. TEAR Fund had been happy to go ahead with my proposal for a mail order business, and their acceptance meant that the base of operation was about to change from London to the North-East.

Two days before Christmas 1974, Tearcraft was registered as a business name of Agrofax Ltd. Agrofax would take over the handicraft stock, and TEAR Fund would produce a mail-order catalogue to send to its list of seven thousand supporters. Extra money was being provided by TEAR Fund to set up the business, and any surplus would return to it after expenses had been met. I had put forward this proposal with plans for expanding Tearcraft into an alternative trading organization. Here was a chance to reach large numbers of people with a message about justice in trade that benefitted producers, employees and customers alike. It was an opportunity to operate a business that had potential for substantial growth in a radically Christian way.

In some ways it was a fresh start. Agrofax had experienced many of the problems that hit small businesses. We had struggled to raise sufficient money in the first place and still had all our capital tied up; in addition we had a large bank overdraft supported by our personal guarantees. We had gone into a specialist business with good intentions but little experience and had bought our training at the price of costly mistakes. Although we had good accountants and solicitors the nature of the business was outside their experience, and often we had to make key decisions without any appropriate advice. Agrofax was at the point where it was only just staying afloat in spite of a lot of hard work from us.

We were continuing to import several tonnes of vegetables each week, but we were still trying to make up for a major loss that had happened earlier in the year. Around Easter the price of green peppers, or capsicums, had gone right down in Kenya. We received one large shipment and were able to sell it at a good price, so we cabled Nairobi for more. Over a week we received about five tonnes of green peppers, but then the price we could ask in the UK was starting to fall, and by the time our cable cancelling further shipments was received another seven tonnes were on the way. We just could not place enough of them around the markets, and soon the smell of rotting 'caps' was hanging over our block of shops. We needed to get rid of them, but none of the local rubbish tips really liked green-grocers' waste. In desperation, we established something that we called 'the death run'.

We would load up the van with putrid stock, covering the top layer with inoffensive empty boxes. One of us would crouch in the back while the other would drive to the Rayner's Lane tip. At the entrance the driver would give the custodian a cheery wave and speed along to the remotest spot. Before the van had come to rest the person in the back would fling open the doors and fling out the rotting material. With luck we would have it all out and be driving off before we could be stopped. One day they must have been waiting for us. As we slopped out our crates of mouldy courgettes and brown and black capsi-cums, two refuse officials appeared. 'Come on, put it all back. We've been watching you lot.' Later that day we returned home covered in vegetable slime having eventually paid to dispose of our smelly waste at a free-enterprise tip where the officials were not so fussy.

The pepper glut put the business in the red. Mike's family, who were involved in the supply end from Kenya, felt that we could have told them to stop sending earlier. We eventually got it all sorted out, not without some loss to all concerned, and the result was that Chris and I now owned all of Agrofax.

Handicrafts enabled us to run down the vegetable-importing side and later dispose of the greengrocer's shop. Meanwhile in Newcastle all was going well. Orders began to arrive in response to the catalogue that went out during February. We were still living in London, but I was getting to know the road to the North well as I ferried up extra shipments of jute crafts. These were stored under the gym of the junior school just over the road from Ray's house. The floor area of this improvised warehouse was large but the ceiling was only four feet high. Throughout it was pitch black and very grimy. It seemed to have some of the characteristics of the local coal mines that were being closed down at the time.

Later, as Ray and I sat in his basement stuffing jute turtles with foam chips, I expressed my surprise over the way things seemed to be developing. 'Look Ray,' I said, 'would you give £10,000 to someone you'd just met that afternoon, let him use your organization's name for his business and then fork out another £3,000 on top to keep things going?' 'It's the old boy network,' explained Ray. 'You know the right people, make the right noises, and they think you are a sound Evangelical. Good job they don't know the truth!'

The opportunity that I had been given to purchase a planeload of handicrafts now provided the right challenges to help me establish a crafts marketing business. We simply had to sell the vast amount of stock. Major policy decisions that were to have far-reaching effects were rushed through, a business was set up at the other end of the country and a pattern of trading that was to last some years was established. It was an opportunity to employ substantial resources with the endorsement of a rapidly-growing Christian development organization. I was immensely grateful for the trust that had been shown in me. George Hoffman was the charismatic and entrepreneurial leader of TEAR Fund and, as he was prepared to back his own judgment to the hilt, he expected similar support in return. But I was already wondering how our relationship would develop, for I suspected that TEAR Fund and I had somewhat different agendas.

I had never been much of a theologian, but had felt for some time that my faith had to be one that I could explain to people without using 'religious' language. My enthusiasm for plain language was probably a legacy from the past. As a choirboy I had enjoyed the singing, but after one attempt to make sense of the rest of the service, I subsequently made sure that I had a book in my cassock pocket. *Gulliver's Travels* was particularly good, I remember. When I was fourteen I began two years of bible study with Jehovah's Witnesses, but again the teaching did not seem to make sense. I took religious education for 'O' level, hoping that the course would provide me with the information I lacked, but I could not take the stuff about the dragon and Armageddon seriously, nor could I understand why teachers insisted on renaming the cross the 'torture stake'.

The theology of the Jehovah's Witnesses I knew left me puzzled, but their commitment impressed me a great deal. One night my study pair arrived at the door literally bleeding. They had crashed on their scooter, but still insisted on explaining why Satan had been released in 1914. I began looking for another perspective on Christian belief itself and decided to go to St Martin's-in-the-Bull Ring, a church situated a few miles away from home, in the centre of Birmingham. St Martin's was a liberal evangelical church whose rector, Canon Bryan Green, drove a 1920s Rolls Royce and smoked incessantly using a long black cigarette holder! He was also a fantastic preacher. His preaching tolerated no nonsense, did not dodge difficult questions, and was down to earth. Through him I came to a faith that was focused on the person of Jesus and that I could defend with arguments based on reason.

By some accident of time and circumstance I had encountered little of the preoccupation with sin that seemed to bother many believing Christians and I had not picked up their jargon. At the university Christian Union I got the distinct impression that faith was there to be defended rather than explored. After 'O' level I had gone on to do 'A' level and was now surreptitiously completing a correspondence-course diploma in theology from London University alongside my sociology degree. How could anyone not be impressed, I wondered, by the resilience and relevance of a faith that could still be so alive and powerful after all that its opponents, but more particularly its defenders, had tried to do to it over the centuries?

I was now sensing the same protective attitude that I had encountered in my fellow students in my TEAR Fund partners. 'Our programmes,' George Hoffman patiently explained to me, 'must be in the hands of those who want to bring others to that fullness of life to be found in Jesus.' 'Absolutely,' I agreed, though later events were to show that we had different ideas about whose hands that could include.

I was only visiting Newcastle occasionally at this stage, and Hilary, safely delivered five months previously, was now finding it difficult to keep up with the rising tide of orders. It was not the baby that was the problem: a large sika and basket made an excellent cradle with a stuffed jute turtle as a mattress; it was the sheer volume of work. The local sub post office experienced a spectacular increase in its parcel traffic and sale of stamps. Part-time help had to be brought in, and we would be needing new premises within a very short time. Not only were TEAR Fund supporters proving good customers; we also found that an increasing number of shops wanted to buy from us.

Although the first range had just been launched, plans were laid for a larger, colour catalogue in the autumn. I visited both India and Bangladesh to establish links with new groups of suppliers. For the next seven years I found myself travelling frequently to many types of craft and food producing groups in developing countries. Tearcraft and Traidcraft between them have dealt with over two hundred such organisations in more than thirty countries. I found that most of them had two needs in common.

The first need was for orders. Many community-based programmes had been developed without planning for sales, and once the training courses became effective stock tended to pile up in discouraging amounts. The second, more critical, requirement was design and marketing advice. The Jute Works had been fortunate in getting the services of an excellent designer from New York who ended up spending three years working with the village women on new techniques and products. However, the result of designing products for the Western market was that the workers had little understanding of what they were making. A Canadian volunteer told me about the time she had asked a group of women from the villages to her home in Dhaka. She had noticed that when they went into her dining room there was a lot of surprise and suppressed laughter. 'Can you tell us please, Mrs Peters, why you sit on the table to eat your food?' one of the ladies asked eventually. It emerged that the table mats that had been in production for two years were believed to be for sitting on. When they saw the mats on the table they had a picture of Westerners perched on top of the table on their mats eating dinner.

After that second trip to Bangladesh we began to make active plans to move to Newcastle. All our money had gone into Agrofax, and Building Societies did not regard owners of small, rather shaky businesses as good mortgage risks. We ended up in a borrowed flat at the top of a Gothic mansion that was owned by a mission to the deaf. Having even a borrowed home close to the actual business gave us a breathing space for a few weeks during the summer of 1975, and in that time a lot happened.

Although the first catalogue had done well, TEAR Fund was having to put increasing amounts of money into Tearcraft as stock was built up for the next, much larger catalogue. There was clearly going to be some unease about the extent to which the charity was exposed to commercial risk and I suggested that the time had come for TEAR Fund to take over Tearcraft completely as a formal subsidiary company. I turned down the offer from George of keeping a sizeable personal stake in Tearcraft as I felt that more substantial resources than I could offer would be needed to maintain the momementum. TEAR Fund needed to feel a sense of ownership for Tearcraft in order to give it the nurturing that it would need.

By July I had the formal title of managing director of Tearcraft Ltd. We had constituted a board of directors, which was intended to work as a sub-committee of TEAR Fund. It identified some warehouse premises in the centre of Newcastle into which we could move in September. There was a lot to do to make sure that we were ready to meet the demand we expected from the new catalogue, and most of my time was spent on the mechanics of getting the new warehousing and mail-order operation well established. In the middle of this hectic activity came news that Sheik Mujib, Bangladesh's leader since independence, had been assassinated with all his family in a house a stone's throw from where I had stayed on my visits. Communications were cut with our main partners. Similar problems were to be a recurring feature or our trade relations, for in ten years twenty more coups were mounted.

My whole attention was now turned to the development of

Tearcraft. We achieved much that was positive, but in retrospect it is easy to see that we had all paid too little attention to the objectives and the structure of the company and its relationship to its parent. Although sales were to shoot up dramatically over the next four years it was going to be against a very stormy background.

3

In Search of Justice

In 1975 Tearcraft was taking its first tentative steps into the world of justice in trade. Alternative trading organizations (ATOs) were relatively new, although Agrofax and Tearcraft were by no means the first. Probably this accolade belongs to Self Help, the trading arm of the Mennonite Central Committee in the United States. It began importing on an informal basis in 1947, entirely through links with sister churches in other parts of the world. By 1970 there were eight ATOs with less than £500,000 sales between them. There are now more than fifty such organizations worldwide with combined turnovers in excess of £40 million.

An ATO is a trading and educational organization that aims to benefit the poor in the Third World. It imports foodstuffs and handmade products from developing countries and uses the business of selling them to inform its customers about economic, social and cultural conditions in the Third World as well as issues related to justice in international trade and development. It also tries to adopt for itself a way of working and being accountable that puts people first. This definition has been hammered out over the last ten years and is now widely accepted. However, the business principles that underlie ATOs are not nearly so well accepted.

When Tearcraft began trading Britain was at the end of a period of decolonization. The preceding twenty years had seen the cartographical pink of empire turn to the greens, yellows and blues of independence. Another change had been taking place at home. The people in the 16-25 year age group had become increasingly conscious of international and political issues; in Europe, where the ATO movement was further advanced than it was in Britain, there was a strong emphasis on education and 'politicization'. The trend towards natural, 'craft' products that had started in the 1960s also favoured the growth of ATOs.

Amongst most of the development agencies a serious debate was in progress about what their role should be. Disaster relief was relatively straightforward. There was an immediate and urgent task to be done to save human lives. But facilitating longer-term development by helping people to become independent of aid, build up their own communities and enable their countries to take a dignified place in the world was much more difficult. For the British agencies it was made more difficult still by the restrictions of the charity law under which they operated. Broadly speaking the courts only recognized four 'charitable purposes', which had originally been set out in a statute going back to Elizabethan times. These were the relief of poverty, the advancement of religion, the furtherance of education and purposes beneficial to the community. When the agencies realized that 'justice' was the real key to international development for the poor, they were accused of being political rather than charitable organizations. Nowhere was this problem felt more acutely than in the main church-related agencies: Christian Aid, CAFOD (Catholic Fund for Overseas Development) and TEAR Fund.

However, the root of the problem did not lie either with the agencies or with the charity law but in the churches themselves. The limited perspective of many of the people in church congregations was encapsulated for me by the account of a visitor from a church community group in the Philippines. Sara spent several days on Tyneside and during that time she said she wanted to see something of our own inner-city problems and to share experiences with local churches. One evening a colleague took her to his church's home-group discussion and bible study. He told me later that the first half of the meeting had been on the topic of 'spiritual warfare': how to recognize and deal with temptation. Then the group leader introduced Sara; he mentioned a book he had read about the great things that God was doing in the Philippines, the number of conversions, healing and so on. He then invited Sara to tell everyone of her experiences of God at work.

To my colleague's secret delight she then began to explain about the struggles against corruption and poverty. She said that some Christians were realizing that there was another way of looking at the gospel, a very different way from the one chosen by their Spanish and American colonizers. She told her listeners how her faith was helping to free her from materialism and selfishness and give her the sort of concern for the poor that Jesus had. She told them of the threats from the military and their worries about being attacked by death squads as they tried to let the poor have more control over their own lives.

'But what of the great work being done by the missionaries to your country?' asked the group leader in consternation. 'Oh, yes, I know those missionaries,' said Sara, 'with their cars and drivers and houses that need three servants.' Her comments were very unsettling for that group of ordinary church members. They had welcomed Sara as a fellow Christian, talked to her and heard her tell of her undoubtedly real, almost glowing, faith; yet now they felt that they were being challenged. They had confidently assumed that people in the Third World were grateful for all that we were doing for them. Perhaps they had always implicitly believed that if people came to have a real faith then everything else would be sorted out. 'I think they forgot about her as soon as they could,' said my friend.

There is a common mistake made by socially-aware Christians. It is assuming that we no longer have to demonstrate how the gospel relates to every aspect of life. The church development agencies have learned through bitter experience that many people limit the applicability of the gospel to strictly religious issues and want their contributions to aid the spread of Christianity rather than the spread of social and economic justice. In our own country we often fail to let our Christian beliefs really influence the way we earn and spend our money and the way we regard our economic system. At the time when Tearcraft was getting established, the debate on these issues was just becoming public. The issues were complex and involved politics, faith, work and lifestyle — a powerful and potentially divisive mix. But the debate was not new and had been going on for the entire history of the Christian church.

Most people today, even Christians, would not consider that the church has any particular right to address them either on the nature and purpose of work or their place as an economic unit in society. We will listen more readily, if not sympathetically, to the TUC, the CBI, the Industrial Society, or even politicians. Yet at one time the church was the only institution with something to say about work and economics, and its views were sophisticated and well developed. It held the view that work is not only necessary but, in some way, commanded by God. To live without working is not only against nature: it is also against scripture. In the early days of Christianity it was thought that if you accumulated so much that you did not need to work then you had a problem. Jesus reminded his followers that it would be as hard for a rich person to enter the kingdom of heaven as it would be for a camel to squeeze through the low city gates that were designed to keep them out — an image that would doubtless have amused people greatly. The church fathers had strong views on those with money to lend. Augustine believed that trade turned a man away from God; Jerome said, 'A rich man is either a thief or the son of a thief.' Although the church itself was accumulating great riches, avarice was regarded as a deadly sin and it remained so for 1500 years. In the fourteenth century the theologian Henry of Langenstein wrote, 'He who has enough to satisfy his wants and nevertheless ceaselessly labours to acquire riches, either in order to obtain a higher social position or that subsequently he may have enough to live without labour, or that his sons may become men of wealth and importance — all such are incited by a damnable avarice, sensuality, or pride.'

The theory of the just price supported this general view. Henry also wrote, 'To leave the prices of goods at the discretion of the sellers is to give rein to the cupidity which goads almost all of them to seek excessive gain. He should charge what he must in order to maintain his position, nourish himself suitably in it, and by a reasonable estimate of his expenditure and labour.'

At the time of the Reformation the church's views on economics faced some severe challenges from the secular world. Vast cargoes of precious metals were being brought back from the New World, and new ideas about the importance of 'the nation' prompted governments to support national trade. In addition a professional and sophisticated banking system was being developed, ironically enough, to handle the vast wealth of the church itself.

In a roundabout way the Reformation itself supported a process of secularizing attitudes about wealth and work. Particularly in the churches influenced by Calvin, stress was laid on the duties of one's 'calling' as a fulfilment of the command to love one's neighbour. Demonstrations of charity could be understood as a visible sign of positive election to eternal happiness. For the next three centuries, even up to the last twenty-five years, the various denominations of the one church had less and less to say on social and particularly economic issues. As faith became individualized and more clearly a relationship between God and the believer, so the secular and the spiritual ground became more clearly defined and church and state kept to their own territory.

We can look back and see that secularization gradually took hold of all spheres of life. Hard work, discipline and perhaps a high sense of responsibility became the virtues in an increasingly materialist society. Profit, ability, success and excellence became critical to economic life. Over a period of four hundred years the medieval point of view was turned upside down.

The perspective on wealth also underwent a subtle change. In some churches one of the few remaining hymns of social comment by Charles Wesley is occasionally sung.

Forth in thy name O Lord I go,
My daily labour to pursue . . .

The fourth verse in older hymn-books starts with a subtle warning about the dangers of avarice.

> Protect me from my calling's snare
> And hide my simple heart above.

Traces of this sentiment still remain in the popular religious songs of the mid-eighteenth century, but by the end of the nineteenth century one of the greatest exponents of industrial capitalism, who was very much a man of faith, could say, 'I believe the power to make money is a gift of God . . . to be developed and used to the best of our ability for the good of mankind.' John D. Rockefeller had arrived at the view that still largely holds sway.

The essence of this contemporary view is that wealth itself is morally neutral: it is *how* it is used that is the crucial question for the Christian. There is an increasing concern today about how wealth is derived, an interest in ethical investments, perhaps even an acceptance that there was something inconsistent about the aggression, violence and underhand practices by which the great philanthropists — Carnegie, Rockefeller, Vanderbilt and many more — gained their wealth, but still no fundamental questioning about the nature of wealth itself.

In other words, the protestant idea of a calling to demonstrate neighbourly love has developed into what might be termed an 'achievement ethic'. The eminent Catholic theologian Hans Kung expressed this view succinctly.

> Man has been attempting to realise himself in a dynamically developing world. Now it is only by *achieving* something that a person *is* something. The worst thing that can be said of anyone is that he has achieved nothing. Work, career, earning money — what could be more important? Industrializing, producing, expanding, consuming on a large scale or a small scale, growth, progress, perfection, improvement in living standards in every respect: is not this the meaning of life? How is man to justify his existence if not by achievements?

This analysis is very much in the style of the moment in popular management and business theory. One of the recent influential management texts, written in 1982, is *In Search of Excellence* by Peters and Waterman. The authors analyze the factors that make the most successful companies what they are, and it is striking that social, ethical or altruistic objectives rarely feature in the mission statements of the top corporations. (The current fashion for top corporations to develop mission statements is perhaps because that phrase effectively combines the religious commitment and military subservience that management requires of its workers.) This omission is also apparent in the 1984 book *The Winning Streak*, subtitled 'Britain's top companies reveal their formulas for success'. And with each month that passes the business and management sections of the bookshops display new titles like *Assess Your Own Achievement Potential, Enterprise and Achievement* and *High Achiever's Handbook*. It would be foolish to dismiss this achievement-oriented approach out of hand, as there is much to be learned from it; but fundamental questions about what constitutes success do need to be asked. These questions alone can challenge the following words from the mission statement of top-performing advertising agency Saatchi and Saatchi, now the largest in the world.

What is fundamental to all these approaches is a belief in excellence . . . all our standards are set by the 'norm': whatever that is, by definition, there is a better way. This has been the fundamental spur to our growth over the years. In all spheres of life and at all times there will be a few performances which are excellent, a few which are poor, whilst the majority will be just average. Our aim in all our activities and at all times is the avoidance of the average and the achievement of excellence.

That is quite a clarion call. But should we not be at least mildly suspicious about the advocacy of excellence from the mouths of the high priests of materialism? Its very appeal seems to spring from the fact that, as human beings, we seem to have a natural yearning for what is good and true. Perhaps the work ethic is

44

not so far from religious thinking as we have been suggesting. I think we have to take another look.

In 1904, in his great work entitled *The Protestant Ethic and the Spirit of Capitalism,* the German sociologist Max Weber wrote: 'Today the spirit of religious asceticism . . . has escaped from the cage . . . and the idea of duty in one's calling prowls about in our lives like the ghost of dead religious beliefs.' More than eighty years on we can recognize that the spirit of excellence and achievement, as well as the populist political spirit of enterprise, are still linked with a semi-religious view of the sanctity of work, and that the concept of the calling is now incorporated into much current management theory. These attitudes have percolated through into political and social life. One of the side effects has been to elevate acquisitiveness from the grubby hole where it crouched as a private vice into the marketplace where it is proclaimed as a public virtue. Business excellence is the new commandment; its rewards are financial and social success.

All this might seem like a long digression from the way church agencies were seeking to tackle issues of poverty, injustice and how to change people's attitudes in the mid seventies. In fact those years were crucial ones when those of us in the development underworld were realizing that the public needed to deal with those issues as part of their everyday expenditure, not by making special charitable contributions from their surplus. Just at this point the economic and political tide turned: business was increasingly thought of as having its own, highly-efficient logic that must be allowed to operate. The needs of the destitute and economically oppressed would eventually be met by this process, but in the meantime relief could be provided by charity from the surplus that those benefitting from the system earned.

So powerful has this movement been that economists have to listen to its strident message, and it is difficult to hear a voice that does not have the hard twang of the enterprise culture. Harvey Cox noted this phenomenon as early as 1965 in has analysis of secularization, *The Secular City.*

We can produce enough for everyone and we believe, or we say we do, that everyone is entitled to a decent share in the productivity of the economy. But we cannot put our convictions into practice in this case because we still feel that only by providing a market-determined job for everyone can the ludicrous imbalance between production and distribution be reconciled.

My dissatisfaction with the current emphasis on excellence, achievement, enterprise and all the other qualities that are linked with work and business does not mean that they should be condemned. Rather they need to be set in their rightful place, which must be firmly anchored in a moral framework. Otherwise, the ethical values that these concepts implicitly carry risk being abused. A Christian moral framework must be based on an understanding of the person of Jesus, not a hotch-potch of institutional and received wisdom. Some of the church agencies were trying to develop such a framework and were coming up with some very radical views on justice and global and national economics as a result. It was clear that these views would not command wide public support if put forward in the programmes of the agencies.

Nevertheless Tearcraft proved to be in a position to put forward an alternative view of trade. As the orders from the first catalogue came in so did the comments. 'How nice to be able to offer people something rather than just ask them for money all the time.' 'I feel that I have a different relationship with the person who made the basket. I want the thing that they made, it seems much more equal.' 'At last I can show my friends that the people in the Third World are skilled and creative.'

As well as stimulating these new perspectives on aid and development, Tearcraft seemed to be attracting wide support reaching far beyond the constituency of its parent. Left-wing bookshops and student groups bought products and applauded our efforts at solidarity with those struggling against oppressive working conditions; we were commended from the other end of the political spectrum for enabling people to 'stand on their own two feet and become self-reliant and not depend on hand-outs.' We had large department stores as customers and enquiries from big catalogue groups. We soon had 'voluntary representatives' registered from every major church denomination and most of the smaller ones. Within a few months Tearcraft became deeply involved in practical ecumenism. Organizations for the young and for the elderly signed up; people used the products for all types of causes from raising funds for their church hall to supporting reconstruction in Hanoi. Even in its earliest days Tearcraft had been able to provide a new, practical method of Third World support that people could adopt in their own way, at their own level and, not infrequently, for their own ends.

One of the things that had deterred me from going ahead with training to become an Anglican minister was the very weight and apparent immovability of the church as a structure. Yet we need structures. As individuals we are weak, prone to error and lacking in resources. People have a desire to be allied to something of permanence and substance. The structures they create to deal with their individual weaknesses tend to acquire a life of their own and a vast inertia, whatever the good intentions of their founders. The tensions of being in perpetual revolution, if that is what the far-seeing organization decrees for itself as a preventive measure, become destructive. At this point the time has come to start again. The organization itself cannot make this move: it is up to the individuals within it to take the initiative and branch out. Tearcraft enabled people to take a new course.

One of the essential features of in its appeal was the sense that people were 'doing something'. Tearcraft, in a very small way, was providing an antidote to the frustration that they felt about the scale of poverty, a problem that many people had seen greatly reduced in Britain in their own lifetime. In 1944, at the same time as the Beveridge Report which was instrumental in establishing the British Welfare State was produced, a conference at Bretton Woods in New Hampshire set up both the World Bank and the International Monetary Fund. At that time it was still possible to believe that the capitalist system, which had enabled first Britain, then Germany, the United States and many European countries to escape the pressure of primitive poverty, could alleviate economic problems in the rest of the world. Although Japan and South Korea may have been successful in this respect, they were exceptions that did not prove the rule. Our economic systems seemed to be structured in favour of the rich and against the poor.

There was another current of thinking that was gaining strength in the early years of Tearcraft. People in the churches were becoming aware that materialism had got the better of us and were asking themselves what constituted a reasonable standard of living so that they would have a larger surplus to redistribute to the poor. This attitude offered the possibility for a two-stage solution to poverty.

The first would be the immediate relief of poverty itself. You might think that people would not voluntarily accept a drop in their standard of living, but consider this analogy. In this story you have to imagine a world where, to set right a major injustice, the people of many nations, almost without protest, accepted punitive rates of taxation and were organized into a massive training and production programme. Soon skilled, semi-skilled and unskilled operatives from one country were at work in other countries; soon ships, heavy transport and aircraft, themselves the result of rapid production programmes, were delivering the fruit of more industrial activity onto the soil of other nations. Billions of pounds flowed, and almost everyone was enthusiastically caught up in the effort. Phenomenal personal sacrifices were made. The shape of countries changed almost overnight. In fact all this actually happened. It was, of course, the Second World War.

What a shame that all that creative energy was turned to destruction. Can you imagine the beneficial results if the resources employed in the Second World War had been employed directly against poverty, disease and ignorance? It is not even necessary to raise the issue of diverting the money that we spend on arms to close that gap between rich and poor. If we merely diverted all the money that the rich nations spend on advertising in a couple of years, or six months' worldwide expenditure on electronic entertainment devices, or two months' expenditure on automobiles we could make great changes. Any of these options would free enough basic resources to abolish the most desperate poverty in our world. If we did want to divert some of our arms expenditure then two or three weeks' worth would be sufficient. Could it be done? The experience of World War II would suggest that it could and that it would create more jobs all round.

Then the longer-term programme would need to be set in place: making a fundamental change in our global economy to give fair trading conditions to all and down-scaling the lifestyle of the rich 20 per cent to create a sustainable future for our planet.

What stands in the way of this solution is that the those of us who are wealthy do not see the pressing need. As a result, the political will is lacking: it is not our national survival that is at stake, it is not our children that are dying and it is not our farming land that is turning to desert. The reality is that we have the capacity to help those who are in need but not the will. The ATOs and the development agencies recognize that their contribution is insignificant in practical terms, but we all have a glimpse of that growing sector of the general public who are appreciating that justice in our global economic institutions and mechanisms is the way that the poor will be saved.

Christians too are coming to accept that no longer can they talk of salvation in purely spiritual, other-worldly terms. The last parable that Jesus told before his arrest and crucifixion was that of the sheep and the goats. It's almost as if he were saying, 'If you remember nothing else, remember this.' And for those of us who are Christians it is an ever-present challenge, for it reminds us of things that have not changed and of actions that are well within our capacities. It brings us back to the here and now for it means feeding the hungry, giving drink to the thirsty, housing the stranger and all those other uncomfortable things.

We are being made to see that salvation is tied in with how we treat our fellow human beings. And as we become more aware of these things so we reclaim the ground that the church has relinquished over the last five hundred years. We need to reclaim it because our concepts of work, wealth, justice, and equity have become fragmented and can only be made whole by relating them all back to God. We need to talk about what must be done, but we can only reclaim the church's involvement in matters of social justice by action, sacrifice, and changing our preconceptions about the lifestyle and the level of wealth we deserve.

We must be aware that we may have to part company with some close friends when we adopt a view that is, at root, highly critical of many attitudes that are woven into the fabric of our society. Our church institutions, national and local, are wedded to a view of responsible stewardship in which there is no place for selling all that we have and following Jesus. We may be able to denigrate the profligacy of the jet set but can we mock the pretensions of the middle class? On what do we base our standard for achievement: business excellence or, as the medieval church would have said, the imitation of Christ? Consider the temptations that Jesus warned us about. In Mark's Gospel you may like to count the number of times that Jesus warns against specific sins. Deceit, indecency, jealousy, pride, folly, pettiness, and cheating all get one mention. Murder, theft, slander and adultery get two. Lack of faith and practising harmful social or religious customs score five each. Status seeking rates seven warnings, but top of the list with twelve very heavy condemnations comes possessiveness and avarice.

Our world is little different in some ways from that of 2,000 years ago. According to best estimates there were some 300 million people populating the entire globe in the first century AD. In spite of our technological progress there are at this moment at least 1,000 million people who live in poverty as bad or worse as any that Jesus would have known. This, for the Christian, must be symptomatic of the continuing triumph of sin. Jesus gives us a personal mission statement which demands a total realignment of our selves, a goal in which conventional achievement has no place, where material values are discarded and where service, not excellence, is the final criterion for judgment.

4

Painful Birth

An old key-cutting machine lay in the middle of the floor covered in dust and a mounted set of italic keys was propped up by the wall. Otherwise the building was empty. Ray Skinner and I were in the middle of a hunt for new premises for Tearcraft and had come to a warehouse in Carliol Square in Newcastle. It had been built in the 1920s in the place where the the old, fortress-like Carliol Gaol had been demolished.

Industrial property was plentiful in the North-East, and more was coming on the market every day as the economic situation worsened and companies retreated to their head offices in the South. We had already been spoiled for choice, but this first-floor warehouse with a goods lift, offices and 1,500 square feet of storage space seemed ideal. It was only 500 yards from the centre of town and even had one or two parking spaces. At £40 a week it was very reasonably priced. We took it and made plans to complete the move so that we would be ready to handle the anticipated rush of orders in the autumn. Tearcraft now had two full-time employees: myself and Bob Foreman, who had just been appointed warehouse manager. Bob had been running his own wholesale business, but had sold it because he had serious reservations about distributing cigarettes. He must have wondered just what he was letting himself in for when he came for an interview in our basement. It must have been a relief for him to discover within a few weeks of joining us that we were moving to a real warehouse and could put a nameplate outside the door like any proper company.

A new colour catalogue replaced the sepia-tinted version and it proved very popular. Several new staff were taken on to cope with the Christmas rush. When, in January, we had time to draw breath, we discovered that we had sold more than £100,000 of products. The Christmas peak is a mixed blessing for any mail-order company. Piling up the orders that arrive in the morning post is a pleasure second only to the music of the cash register in a busy shop. Tempering the excitement is the concern that there might not be enough stock. We were not in a position to phone our suppliers and ask them to put extra deliveries on a lorry to us the following week. We had placed most of our orders nine months before the goods were sold. Production took three months and sea freight another three. There was no way of getting goods in a hurry so we had to be right in our estimates first time. Needless to say we ran out of stock in many products, and even now, with many years' experience of forecasting, miscalculations still occur.

Another mixed blessing was the attention of the press. The curious sight of lorry-loads of jute bales arriving in the middle of Newcastle attracted the media, and we were soon getting regular coverage in the local newspapers. The pattern was fairly standard. 'Let me heap you up with all these bags and string things,' the photographer would say, 'and then you can stand beside the name plate, and make sure you smile.' A few days later a headline of the 'Full of eastern promise' variety would announce a story that was meagre on facts and heavy on human interest. The following appeared in the Newcastle *Evening Chronicle* in May 1976.

It's six years since Richard Adams was living in Newcastle and working hard to promote the industrial potential of the region as an assistant industrial development officer with the North-East Development Council. Now he's back, but this time selling the cottage industries of India and Bangladesh.

In the years between he moved to London to set up his own import business, bringing exotic fresh vegetables and fruit from the developing countries to sell at Covent Garden. Then a brand-new idea brought a new business venture and the chance to return to Tyneside with his wife and two young children.

The strategy was simple. Form a mail order company which would market handicrafts produced in the villages and back streets throughout India and Bangladesh. Soon it is hoped to include Haiti and Swaziland. Behind the plan was The Evangelical Alliance Relief Fund, a mouthful of a name which contributed its initials to give the venture a name — Tearcraft. It was felt that by buying the products of needy countries, giving the craftsmen a fair price for their work then selling it in Britain on a commercial basis, much good could be done for the village economy of poor nations.

But one thing Richard Adams stresses is that Tearcraft is not a charity: it's a business. Based in Carliol Square it sells a range of almost 100 products through its mail order catalogue. Richard says he is involved because of his own links with the church. At one time he was at St John's College, Durham, and thinking of being a minister. But he opted for ten years in the business world and his work with Tearcraft is a perfect combination of the two commitments. There is a team of eight people who care about their work and see its appeal to the general public who, in an economic crisis, are glad they can buy something useful and help someone at the same time.

Everything is sold at the lowest possible price and the more that is sold the more jobs are created, and that's the object of the exercise. To date about 1,000 jobs have already been provided by the goods that Tearcraft has already sold.

That story was the first, and it was typical of many features that Tearcraft and later Traidcraft would get in the local and national press. The issues about jobs, prices, helping the poor and the good working atmosphere in the company were usually well covered, but invariably there were two omissions. Right from the beginning I was keen to stress that our bargain is someone else's raw deal, and that our intention was not merely to make the business system better but to establish a new system that based on a different set of values.

The first point is a difficult one. We are conditioned to believe that lower prices are an indication of business efficiency. The link is a valid one, and in a perfect market where there is equal opportunity and power it does work well. The price of potatoes provides a good example. Farmers only grow potatoes when they can expect to get a good price for the crop, and if the price falls they switch to a different crop. Consumers only buy from shops that offer the produce at a reasonable price and will readily switch to shops where the price is lower if necessary. There are lots of growers, lots of shops and lots of buyers. The mechanism is self-regulating, although the price of potatoes varies considerably with the season and the weather.

The factors affecting the supply of cane baskets are rather different. Of course there are lots of baskets available from countries all over the world, so the buyer has a good choice. However, the Bangladeshi craftworkers who make cane baskets simply cannot switch to another product when prices fall. Cane is their only raw material and making baskets is a traditional skill learned over the years. The people are not unwilling to change, but they have few real options. Who will provide the money for any new investment needed, and what are they going to live on while they are learning a new skill? Many people in the Third World, and not a few in our own country, are in this position. They have little power to direct the economy to their advantage and are easily exploited.

I came across an example of this sort of exploitation in the course of two visits I made to Bangladesh in late 1975 and early 1976. Tearcraft was gathering momentum, and whilst I was building up relations with the Jute Works and other agencies I continued to look out for new products. In November 1975 I visited a very impressive operation with a big office in

Dhaka. The company, which was based in the United States, was producing crewel kits. These wool-on-canvas tapestries were sold in America 95 per cent finished. All the purchaser had to do was stitch in a few of the more interesting details with the wool provided and claim the work as original. There was, apparently, a big demand. The company had begun by having the embroidery done in America; first it switched to South Korea and then, as wage rates increased, to South Vietnam. Some local difficulties for America in that area had forced a prompt removal, this time to Bangladesh.

In all cases it was village women who were involved. They were loaned money by the company so that they could buy a month's supply of materials. They completed their task, returned the almost-finished picture of a teddy bear or giant redwood and received about double the cost of the materials. In the first month, if all went well, they could clear their debt; in the second month they could easily earn as much as their husbands would be getting as agricultural labourers — about £11 a month. Many of the skilled jute producers switched over to this work. Some found the work very lucrative, although there were problems: if the picture got dirty, or if the children played with the material, or if the goat ate it, then no payment was forthcoming. Nevertheless, large numbers of workers were being attracted to this high-paying work away from cooperatives that had taken years to establish.

When I returned three months later the crewel company was gone. It had been offered a tax-free deal by the government in the Philippines and had taken the offer with no regard for the local workers. Several thousand women were left without work; several thousand families suffered a drastic fall in living standards and could do nothing about it. I have frequently encountered international companies, both large and small, who are constantly chasing the best deal across the world and leaving a trail of unfulfilled expectations and wasted experience or training behind. Developing countries are encouraged to be competitive with each other to win the favours of these companies, but often it is their own people who end up being exploited. This is the price that we pay for using a system where profit, price and efficiency are the overriding values.

In the final analysis this type of system exists because we, as customers and consumers, support it. From time to time, however, indivduals choose to operate in a different way. Their compassion has led the well-known American conservative economist Milton Friedman to say: 'Few trends could so thoroughly undermine the very foundation of our free society as the acceptance by corporate officials of a social responsibility other than to make as much money for their shareholders as possible.' My experience with Agrofax and our growing understanding of the mechanisms of trade through Tearcraft helped me to see what many development agencies we recognizing: that you cannot keep politics out of charity. Relationships with TEAR Fund were also showing that you cannot keep politics out of religion either.

One incident brought this issue to the fore. It happened when the actual supply of cane baskets from Bangladesh was insufficient to meet the demand generated by out colour catalogue. We sold these baskets to fit in the macramé sikas that were our best line, with hundreds being sold each week. To keep sales going I had hunted around British wholesalers and found a supply of the necessary round-bottomed baskets at a firm in Lancashire. I was not so naive as to think that the label saying 'People's Republic of China' was going to be an asset. I phoned TEAR Fund and explained the problem, and together we agreed that if we could remove the labels and send these baskets to trade customers only, we could go ahead. The inevitable happened: some labels were missed, and some baskets were sent to a TEAR Fund supporter who equated Mao with Nero. We were in trouble.

About this time TEAR Fund was under pressure from two directions. The evangelical missionary societies saw the growth of the Christian 'relief and development' sector as siphoning off funds from conventional missionary work; their own supporters were concerned to see greater links between evangelism, support for local Christians and humanitarian aid. Indeed, TEAR Fund had just decided to bring people's attention to the issue of help for oppressed Christians in Eastern Europe. The popularity of the John le Carré spy stories added a certain glamour to this area, but many of the organization's supporters were unwilling to go any further in helping countries that had socialist or communist governments.

In these various ways politics came onto the agenda. The senior staff at TEAR Fund recognized the need for dealing with the issue, but they feared a loss of support if they moved away from their traditional position of ignoring politics. By now I was certain in my own mind that if I wanted to act as a responsible member of what Jesus referred to as God's kingdom, I had to tackle political and social issues even if involved pointing out the flaws in the capitalist system that operated in Britain. I knew that there would be tensions, but I could not ignore the problems.

At the same time, the church in the West was laying increasing emphasis on the judgmental and retributive aspects of God and appeared to growing less tolerant of variations in belief. In politics, too, the shift was away from social concern and in favour of individual initiative. TEAR Fund and Tearcraft were concerned not alienate the increasing numbers of people who endorsed such views. Their caution made it difficult for me to work with them.

Tearcraft itself was going from strength to strength. After the first season we took a second floor in the warehouse building. For the Christmas period in 1976 we employed twelve people. During the year we had been joined by Michael Shaw, who accepted a 25 per cent cut in salary to move from being administration manager at the nearby Ever Ready battery factory. Michael, like Bob Foreman, had been looking for a job in which he could relate his faith to his work; indeed, the concern to do business in an ethical way was a feeling we all shared. We certainly had something to aim for, especially as the goods we handled each day reminded us of people in the Third World. Every week we extended a coffee break to learn more about the people on whose behalf we were working. The session would sometimes take the form of a slide show and might be followed by a discussion about the causes of poverty. We invited visitors from overseas to speak to us about their perspectives and would also invite local staff from development agencies in to tell us about their work. But this was just one aspect of our exploration of what it meant to make faith and work interdependent.

My own experience of management until then had been fairly limited, but I had learned that the more people were informed about their work, the more they felt involved and the more effectively would they contribute. I was keen to establish a policy of openness and participation in Tearcraft, and to this end provided talks about how the business was run, how we put budgets together, the criteria we used for selecting new staff and how we determined appropriate wage levels. We had an equal benefits policy for all staff. Perks, such as they were, applied to all staff equally. These ranged from free coffee and tea at breaks to a generous non-contributory pension. Our salaries were fixed in a ratio of the highest not being more than twice the lowest, and even the lowest was fixed at a good rate for the area. As a result, the salaries of lower-paid staff were above average whilst the higher-paid accepted less than they might have got elsewhere.

We were still small enough for everyone to sit in a comfortable circle at break-time, and this approach is certainly the most effective form of staff communication in business yet devised. Everyone joined in the work of unloading a shipment or putting out a mailing, and in the busy season everyone helped to pack. There was a price to be paid for the friendly working atmosphere, however: it encouraged people to be more open about their own personal problems and concerns. As we unloaded a particularly difficult shipment of heavy wooden crates without benefit of a fork-lift truck Michael Shaw said, 'That's one of the interesting things about Tearcraft: you can never tell at the start of the day whether you're going to be a labourer or a social worker.'

Our family circumstances had changed yet again. Lewis had been born a true Geordie within sight of the Tyne. A few weeks later we made our eighth move in seven years, joining Ray and Hilary in their new home, an extremely large vicarage built in the Victorian Gothic style in Newbottle, an ex-mining village about ten miles south of Newcastle. Ray had been appointed a director of Tearcraft in 1975 and he provided very effective local support for both myself and the rest of the staff as all the other directors appointed by TEAR Fund were in the South-East.

The third Tearcraft catalogue came out in the autumn of 1976 and helped sales to reach £180,000. We had taken space at some trade fairs during 1976, and about 30 per cent of turn-over was now through wholesalers and retail shops. I felt that this strictly commercial interest in our wares was particularly encouraging for the producers who could be assured that people were not just buying their goods from a charitable impulse. We had advertised the catalogue in *Good Housekeeping* and *Reader's Digest*, and the result was nearly 6,000 requests in a ten-day period. Once again I detected some concern from TEAR Fund, who had never advertised or promoted their work outside the Christian press. Our view was that we had a responsibility to our partners in the Third World to find as large a market as possible for what they were making.

Space was again proving a problem. We were able to rent another vacant floor in an adjoining building. Although there was no direct route between our original base and the new stor-age area we could move bales between them via the fire escape and a toilet window. This became a regular route until someone dropped a bale of Chandpur placemats, which crashed onto a car that was parked beneath. The roof of the car was seriously dented, and it was extremely fortunate that there was no one inside it.

The variety of goods we were handling was increasing. Pro-jects in Thailand, the Philippines, Sri Lanka, Kenya, Malawi and Haiti were now represented. With the new products came some unforeseen problems. Some of the attractive bead necklaces turned out to be made of lethal seeds; bamboo beetles, termites and mildew made frequent appearances, and we imported a whole family of Indian mice in a shipment of embroidered cushion covers. The fauna of central Newcastle was enriched by some exotic immigrants, as no one had the heart to exterminate the travellers.

At the beginning of 1977 we were joined by Jan Simmonds, Chris' best friend from college, who had been working as a careers officer. Jan became Tearcraft's information officer, producing materials for our 100 voluntary representatives, most of whom were based in churches around the country. About the same time we held our first national conference at an inner-city church in Birmingham. More than 120 people attended and demonstrated such interest that we decided to spend more money on encouraging our volunteers. The first voluntary representatives had selected themselves after receiving the initial catalogue. 'Can we buy in bulk? Is there more information about the groups? Have you any posters?' were the questions they asked. We realized that we had a keen and willing sales force who just needed a little encouragement. This group of people was to become the mainstay of both Tearcraft and Traidcraft, not only by the sales they generated but also because of the excellent job they were to do in telling people about justice in trade. People could relate more easily to this issue when they saw how their pattern of living and choice of spending could affect someone on the other side of the globe.

We needed to begin preparations for a new range of products at least nine months in advance and, in addition to managing a rapidly-growing company, I was still doing all the travelling to groups, selection of products and compilation of the catalogue. Although most of Tearcraft's literature was produced by TEAR Fund, it was becoming more difficult to liaise with designers and photographers in London in order to present our increasing range of goods. In 1977 we decided to base the catalogue production in Newcastle, and to this end we set up a small photographic studio in a corner of the warehouse. We had always proceeded on a do-it-yourself basis, not least because our premises were so dilapidated that we had decided to our own maintenance person. As we grew we added in-house facilities that helped to make us more self-contained and also gave us practical experience that we could usefully pass on to our producer partners.

During the year our sales doubled to £370,000. We now had twenty-five permanent staff, almost as many as in the TEAR Fund headquarters in Teddington. We again needed more space and discovered that the adjoining warehouse building was about to come on the market. We persuaded TEAR Fund that it would be a good investment, and actually bought the four-storey premises, most of which had not been altered since it was built in 1930. We now had a total of thirty thousand square feet of space costing us, including rates, about £25,000 a year. Glyn MacAulay, the Tearcraft non-executive chairman, who had been TEAR Fund's first chairman for seven years, frequently pointed out that we would be lucky to rent three medium-sized offices in the City of London for that price.

We were now able to establish well-planned rows of bins and storage racking, a repair section, an attractive rest area and canteen under the top floor lantern-light roof, and group together our growing range of 'high-tech' equipment. With much debate about the possible effect on jobs we had bought sophisticated mail-out equipment, installed Telex and switched to electric typewriters. We were still in the process of deciding whether or not to replace our electro-mechanical accounting machines with computers. Although this level of automation sounds very basic today it was quite innovative for a company our size at that time. TEAR Fund staff who visited us were quite envious, and their response highlighted for me the advantage that we had as a trading company.

Tearcraft produced yearly accounts as a subsidiary of TEAR Fund in accordance with the law. We had shown break-even or modest surpluses since we started. Conventional accounting methods resulting in a balance sheet and profit-and-loss account are an excellent way of assessing business efficiency. Of greater importance, however, are the objectives of the company. Tearcraft did not aim to maximize its profits, unlike some charity shops. Our work in fair trade and producer support was the end in itself, although of course we needed to run profitably whilst doing the work. The main drain on TEAR Fund resources was the capital that was required to purchase stock and to buy the buildings and equipment we needed to run a business. However, TEAR Fund's investment in us generated a much larger flow of cash out to the Third World in payment for goods than straightforward charitable giving. At the same time, selling crafts provided TEAR Fund supporters with a new type of outlet through which to promote the need for giving.

61

Taken as a whole Tearcraft was a good investment for TEAR Fund and, provided we managed the business efficiently, we could invest in growth and development in a way that a charity found difficult. Charities tend to be assessed by the general public on how much of their overheads are spent on administration and how much money actually goes to 'the cause'. This tends to result in a penny-pinching attitude towards internal expenditure. I have seen major charities working in grossly inefficient conditions because of the psychological difficulty they have in justifying major capital expenditures to improve their administration. At the end of 1977 we could point out to TEAR Fund that although it would have £180,000 invested in Tearcraft by the following year, we would be generating sales of £600,000. About £300,000 of this money would go to the Third World, and we hoped to have an overall profit of £80,000.

Our ability to present detailed financial justification for our activities had taken a big leap forward when Brian Hutchins joined us at the beginning of 1978. Brian had been a voluntary representative when he had first read the job advertisement and he had taken many months to decide to leave his well-paid job in Cumbria and move to Newcastle with his growing family. As a qualified accountant Brian gave Tearcraft the financial expertise it needed at a time when it was doubling in size each year. He was another of the competent managers who was able to provide professional skills at the right time.

When he joined us, however, Brian was far from happy about his decision. He had walked into what was a mounting storm about the degree of independence that Tearcraft could exercise and said later that for months he asked, 'Lord, why have you sent me over here?' The tensions were not new. As early as July 1976, after the 'Red China Basket Incident', Glyn MacAulay had circulated a memo saying, 'This is yet another "misunderstanding" in a long saga of such events. I have told Richard, therefore, that I can see only two alternatives, one is that he in some way manages to take over the whole operation and run it independently or, two, he leaves.' In response I had put forward proposals for dividing the two operations, but at the time we had been able to make up our differences. Now a whole range of new issues were highlighting rift between Tearcraft and its parent body.

The roots of the the problem were complex, but they often focused on the type of producer group we were dealing with. TEAR Fund had always insisted on applying its criteria to Tearcraft's sources of supply. George Hoffman set out TEAR Fund's position to me in a letter of 5 April 1978.

Ideally, of course, we would like to see Tearcraft purchasing solely from groups organized by, or associated with, evangelical Christians. However, we recognize the problems this creates in certain government controlled or ecumenical/humanitarian co-operative enterprises through which Evangelicals have to participate.

We wrote back immediately stating our position. The letter was signed by Bob, Michael, Brian and myself and in itself illustrated another of our differences with TEAR Fund. We had kept the entire staff, who numbered about thirty-two at that time, fully informed about every development; as a result we were able say that we had unanimous support. On the critical issue about suppliers we wrote as follows.

You will be aware that the evangelical world is continuing to look outwards and recognize the contribution that other sections of the church are making to Christian ministry. We regard Tearcraft as a living witness to the movement of the Spirit, combining as it does Baptist, Anglican, Brethren, Roman Catholic, Mennonite and Pentecostal groups in a ministry which has as its objective a Christian response to the physical and social imperatives of the Gospel. We cannot polarize the social and spiritual elements of a Christian ministry but a rigid 'Christian identification' would do just this and must lead to the suspicion that TEAR Fund is more concerned about its supporters than those it supports.

The letter went on to point out that Tearcraft had given TEAR Fund access to people it would otherwise not have contacted and also said that 'Three thousand individuals look to us for continued employment, amongst secular and non-evangelical producing groups who see an evangelical Christian firm acting positively where others have never ventured.'

More than ten years have brought a dramatic change in attitudes, and it is hard to see why these issues were so divisive. At that time, however, both sides were digging in their heels. As painful as these things can be at the time, my own view has always been that tensions, disagreements and strongly-held opinions are bound to result from any form of creative, radical initiative. The problem is increased in Christian organizations that think they have some kind of authority to decide what is right. The only option in the face of such conflict is to find a solution that minimizes the damage. Over the next year we sought to do just that in our relations with TEAR Fund.

This became increasingly difficult. The agenda that I had set for Tearcraft in the Agrofax days was of a comprehensive approach to issues of justice in trade. The organization was a specifically Christian one, but I had never imagined that it would seek to be exclusive or claim a spiritual monopoly. We tried to sell to people who were not Christians and we employed some people who did not have any specific Christian commitment. Moreover, 90 per cent of what we sold was made by people of other religions even though their efforts were channelled through church organizations. A further cause of aggravation then arose.

Jan Simmonds, in her work of developing the voluntary representatives scheme, arranged for one of our most active and committed reps to provide a presentation on Tearcraft at a Baptist church in Surrey. John Ruming is still very active in issues of development, justice and peace. As a matter of courtesy he discussed with the church in advance what he was going to do and the facilities he would need. The next day TEAR Fund received a very strong complaint that it had recommended a Roman Catholic as a speaker. Phones buzzed; Jan was asked to cancel John's visit, which she did. As John was not himself on the phone at that time Jan wrote to him and in her letter added that she was personally sorry to find this degree of intolerance in Christian circles. Copies of all our correspondence were forwarded to TEAR Fund as a matter of course, and as a result this letter was produced at a board meeting. The board called for Jan's instant dismissal.

For more than a year we had discussions about ways to separate Tearcraft from its parent. We began work on forming an independent trust to take over the company and canvassed a broad spectrum of church figures to see whether they would lend their support through endorsement. There were many difficulties. TEAR Fund now had over £200,000 tied up in Tearcraft assets, and we would need money to buy these out. More important was the fact that, in spite of the tensions, the Tearcraft operation had been immensely successful amongst TEAR Fund supporters and beyond. TEAR Fund would be losing a major resource if it sold out. During early 1979 various deals were suggested. Tearcraft staff and the three hundred voluntary reps were inundated with information and questionnaires. Of our thirty-nine staff all but two were supportive of the proposal to separate from TEAR Fund and we knew that many of the voluntary reps, accounting for nearly 40 per cent of our sales, felt the same way.

In the end, however, we just could not reach an acceptable deal. The proposed new trust had raised, or had promises of, £50,000; we proposed to repay the balance owing to TEAR Fund over three years, and during that time TEAR Fund would retain ownership of the stock as security. This option, and other variations, all fell at the last fence. Early in June 1979 I found myself travelling to London with Brian and Michael for the final showdown. TEAR Fund board members and their solicitor agreed with us that we had not been able to reach a scheme for purchasing Tearcraft that was satisfactory to both parties. I then had a separate meeting with the Tearcraft chairman, and much to my surprise was offered a large sum of money as a golden handshake.

'That's very generous, John,' I said, thinking furiously, 'but you will still be left with these awkward producer groups within Tearcraft and the "non-Christian" trade customers. Why not make the cash sum a lot less and offer me a facility to buy

Tearcraft's stock from these groups and give me a start in selling it by transferring the trade customers to me.' John reflected a moment; 'That sounds as if it might work,' he said. 'Let's look at the detail.' Within thirty minutes we had an agreement, which I personally guaranteed, that up to £60,000 of Tearcraft stock from five non-evangelical groups could be sold to the new company, Traidcraft, during the next twelve months at two-thirds of cost price. In addition all the Tearcraft trade customers would be transferred to Traidcraft over two years. I would receive £5,000 and be able to inform the voluntary reps about what was happening. This deal had to be signed by me within two days, at which point I would cease to be Tearcraft's managing director.

We emerged to talk with the larger group. The TEAR Fund solicitor read out the agreement, and I watched the faces around the table. There was relief amongst the TEAR Fund folk and growing amazement from Brian. 'Why did they agree to it?' he asked on the train back to Newcastle. 'What we're getting must be worth at least £50,000 and up until now we've been talking about paying them money?' I wasn't entirely sure. 'Either they were being extremely generous or they think that Traidcraft isn't going to work and it will be the cheapest option.' I wanted to think that it was the former.

5

People before Profit

By the middle of June I was on the dole. I hoped that registering would be a purely precautionary step, but there was still plenty to do before Traidcraft was certain to get off the ground. Preparations had started more than a year previously with the first plans to take over Tearcraft as a going concern. Traidcraft Ltd had been in existence since October 1977 when it started life as a shop in Bristol run by a group of local reps. The shop had now closed so it had been possible to buy the ready-formed company and transfer the shares. In the preceding twelve months I had found the old boy network very useful in bringing together people who were supportive of the new Christian initiative in trade that Traidcraft set out to establish.

John Gladwin, then the director of the Shaftesbury Project but soon to become secretary to the General Synod's Board for Social Responsibility, took on the role of chairman-elect of the Trust. Garth Hewitt, who was rapidly developing his career as a gospel singer and Christian communicator while working with the Church Pastoral Aid Society, and Lionel Holmes from the Bible Medical Missionary Fellowship were also involved in planning and development. They had all been contemporaries with Chris, Jan, Tim and me at university and we later acquired the collective title of the Durham Mafia! The circle widened until we had a large number of people involved in different aspects of Christian work ready to endorse the organization that had originally planned to take over Tearcraft. When the take-over fell through, and it became clear that Tearcraft was going to continue under TEAR Fund with Traidcraft pushing into new areas, only a very few people withdrew, so we were able to build on a lot of goodwill from many influential people within the church.

Over the previous few years I had seen many different organizations at work and had noted their strengths and weaknesses, but had not found a particular model on which to base Traidcraft. The structure was something that we had to get right at the beginning. We were looking for one that could allow the organization to work in the areas of education and campaigning as well as actual trading. At the same time this new organization had to be accountable to an effective, independent group separate from the executives of the company itself. Finally we had the problem of money and power, which are normally strongly linked in a conventional company. How were the two to be separated in Traidcraft so that ideals could be maintained and the interests of producers and customers kept high on the agenda?

It was nearly seven years before the final form was legally fully constituted, and the result was a two-part organization. The first was a charity, the Traidcraft Exchange. The 'objects' of the Exchange were to encourage fair trade with developing countries through education, research, loans, grants and personnel. The Exchange owned virtually all the voting shares in the trading company, the original Traidcraft Ltd, and they therefore had the right to appoint the directors at each annual general meeting. The charity was not involved in the day-to-day running of the company, but was there as a watchdog, ready to step in and use its teeth if the trading side ever strayed from the principles of justice that it had been established to uphold.

The charity obtained its original funds from the money that had been raised to buy out Tearcraft. They were used to buy shares in Traidcraft Ltd to provide starting capital. Most of the £5000 that had been paid to me when I left also went towards the start-up. Seven people moved from Tearcraft to Traidcraft in the first few months, and we split that money equally amongst us to buy Traidcraft shares.

Traidcraft Ltd was an unusual beast. It had a large number of directors, most of them non-executive. They were nominated by the trustees of the charity, by the staff, by the voluntary representatives, and by the Council of Reference, although the power of appointment belonged to the shareholders. The Council of Reference was our list of the great and good: people who endorsed Traidcraft as 'a good thing' and gave others a degree of confidence that we had some substance. We set out to be both ecumenical and accessible to all main Christian traditions and the people on the council reflected some of this diversity, although it was still heavily weighted towards the evangelical wing of the church. Alongside the MPs Alan Beith and Brian Mawhinney were Bruce Kent, John Stott and Simon Barrington-Ward.

A lot of the legal groundwork had been prepared when it was anticipated that Traidcraft would be taking over Tearcraft lock, stock and barrel. Our advance planning gave us time to put our energies into finding new premises and establishing the business as a going concern. In early June we were expecting to have a certain amount of cosmetic work to do in changing our sign, stationery and so on; now we had to develop a new company from scratch and had two months before the peak season in which to do it.

The first task was the production of a catalogue. Economy and speed led to a single-colour, twelve-page booklet with hand-drawn artwork. The colour was light brown, my favourite at the time, and as 95 per cent of the products were the same colour, the rumour developed that I would buy anything so long as it was brown and there was lots of it. Stock was not a problem as we had our agreement with Tearcraft to take more than a hundred lines that they already held from groups that they wanted to phase out of their trading. But where were we going to put it?

Unfortunately for the North-East things had been going from bad to worse economically. As a result there were still plenty of empty warehouse premises available. With a feeling of déjà-vu I began the round of agents. 'We have something on the top floor of a warehouse block in Carliol Square,' the first one said. Just round the corner from Tearcraft about five thousand square feet on the fifth floor had come on the market. It was all we needed to get started. A team of volunteers from a local youth club used brooms, buckets of water and then plenty of white emulsion to make the place habitable. Within six weeks of leaving Tearcraft we were open for business under the Traidcraft name and five others had joined me in what was to be our home for the next four years.

In those first few months business was slow but steady. Our unconventional catalogue had not been a wild success with the new customers we had tried to recruit, but we were receiving regular orders from the 180 voluntary representatives who had decided to give Traidcraft a try as well as Tearcraft. We also were finding that ordinary shops and department stores were still buying jute and cane products though we noticed a slowing down in the demand for sikas, Tearcraft's main product line since it started. At the end of our financial year, after trading for eight months, we had made sales of £123,000 and a surplus (our word for profit) of £12,000. From most points of view it was not a good time to be starting a company. Inflation was galloping, unemployment was growing, the pound was weakening and a report published in the same month that we opened our doors for business recorded that 85 per cent of new businesses went bust in their first year. In the wider world the Brandt report on international development was launched and we elected a new government. Both were to be very significant in determining how Traidcraft approached the issues of poverty, justice and freedom.

Both Brandt and the enterprise culture were concerned with values and both contained radical ideas. There were a surprising number of similarities. Both called for a new approach to deep-seated problems based on an appeal to self-interest; both spelled out the dangers of becoming too dependent; both encouraged people to stand on their own two feet and develop their capacities for enterprise and achievement. What quickly became clear, however, was that Mrs Thatcher's vision for a new Britain was dynamic, action-centred, and, on its own terms, successful, while Brandt struggled to convince the general public that its answers were relevant. For me it was all summed up by the following problem of the electric toaster.

We had listened to an evening of speeches and discussion by politicians, economists and overseas development workers. We had taken the Brandt report apart, praised and criticized it, and recognized it as a major contribution to the debate. Along with four hundred others in Newcastle's sumptuous council chamber I then listened as a woman in her early forties stood up.

'I came here tonight hoping to find an answer to a problem I had last week,' she said. 'I was in town, shopping, and I went into Curry's intending to buy an electric toaster.' The chamber was the quietest it had been all evening. 'But I stopped; I thought about this meeting and said to myself, "I don't really need a new toaster: my old one will probably last a good while longer."' By now we were all identifying with the woman's dilemma. She went on, 'I thought, "Don't get it. Use the money to help the poor in a creative way, in a way that you know will work." But do you know, I couldn't think of what that way might be, and I still haven't heard anything tonight that would have helped me. I bought my new toaster and I know there are millions like me who will do the same unless you can give a more positive lead.'

I have mentioned that incident often enough since then to know that many people have felt the same way. The vast majority of us have seen our standard of living rise consistently over the last thirty years. At the same time we have experienced a subtle inflation in our expectations. Luxuries become necessities, what were special occasions become commonplace, our very affluence seems to find a voice that insistently whispers, 'More, more, more.' This whisper is a particularly irritating one, but we can find relief from it for a short while when we follow its instructions. When we buy the toaster, the camera, the three-piece suite, the foreign holiday, the fitted kitchen, the new car or the house in a better neighbourhood, then it falls silent for a few hours, or days, or even weeks.

Now this pressure to buy, to consume, to be entertained can also be thought of as the background music to our economic life. Marketing has become a highly-specialized technique, and we are up against people who are skilled in an insidious but legal

71

combination of therapy and brainwashing. The laws of supply and demand in a prosperous, competitive economy are fairly simple: the more that is demanded by people who can afford to pay, the more can be supplied. In the best of all worlds it may be acceptable to allow these laws to operate, at least if we can be sure that there are no hidden social costs and if we do not ask whether accumulating things leads to genuine happiness and fulfilment. But our world is far from ideal. We know that our standard of living, which is not the highest in the world by any means, cannot be shared by the billions who still live in the poverty from which we have escaped over the last 250 years. The problem is not their undeniable lack of money; nor is it that they do not work enough, for they labour far harder than people in the wealthy nations. No, it is simply that the earth, our planet, does not have the resources and could not support the effort needed to let everyone live in the way to which *we* have become accustomed.

And it is this knowledge, this appreciation of a basic unfairness, that makes a few people stop and think as they buy their toaster. For others it is the image of the starving children in the Sudan or the floods in Bangladesh seen on last night's television news. Perhaps many people pause, thinking of others less fortunate than themselves. What is certain is that it is only a pause for thought; for most it probably does not lead to action for the poor and disadvantaged.

Now in Britain we are no more heartless than the people of the other eleven countries in the European Community. We are no more selfish than the 1,000 million other individuals in the world's twenty-four major industrialized nations. We all think that we know the needs of the poor because we have had them presented to us by our media and, from time to time, we have responded as requested. We have sent money, delivered envelopes, rattled the collection box, worn red noses, parachuted, marathoned, raffled, covenanted, fasted, lobbied and petitioned. And the poor are still with us. We have played the tune that was asked of us, but the poor have not danced to prosperity and the oppressed still await their freedom. We live in an age of rapid change and progress and our expectations are high, yet here is failure and a world unlike the one we know where billions upon billions given in the form of aid only seem to lead to the next famine. It seems that we have been led astray, that nothing works and that our efforts are pointless. 'After all, I might as well buy that toaster because nothing I can do will make any difference.'

Such a view is, in some respects, a parody of the way people think and it appears to ignore the many achievements of the developing nations in their fight against poverty. But I believe that people accept this view in the same way that they accept that achievement, enterprise, wealth and possessions are the key to a successful life. Both views are parodies, incomplete and over-simplified, but most people are looking for a simple life and are more than happy to accept convenient explanations.

As Traidcraft started trading we realized that we were able to provide some ways in which people had an alternative to buying the toaster. We also realized that what we were offering could be profoundly subversive of the traditional view of the 'market economics' that was gaining increasing support and had been instrumental in winning the recent election.

We were asking people to buy products not because they were cheap or even because they were the best value around but on the understanding that justice and the needs of others were to be considered as part of the buying process alongside price and quality. This approach puzzles economists. After all, people are recognized as being intrinsically selfish and likely to seek out the best bargain for themselves, irrespective of the cost to others. It is this approach that has enabled us to ignore for so long the fact that it is our drive to possess and consume that has often made it difficult for the majority in our world to have that standard of living that our nation achieved four generations ago.

During Traidcraft's first year we all were on the rota for making tea and coffee, just as we shared responsibility for cleaning and some of the other tedious chores. At break time we sat together in our small rest room and talked, mostly about work. It was a very effective way for everyone to keep in touch. As the economics of the marketplace began to be promoted by the new government it dawned on us that the type of market that our leaders had in mind was a very particular one: Mrs Thatcher's market seemed to draw inspiration from the stock market and the supermarket yet traditionally the market, although certainly a place where people came to buy and sell, was far more than that. It had been the centre for a network of human relationships that had more to do with news, sharing, and support than making an efficient profit. A traditional market was a place for renewing friendships and cementing them through mutually satisfactory transactions.

As we talked about this particular issue one day someone said, 'I suppose one person's bargain is another's raw deal.' Eventually we were to use this remark as a campaign slogan, but at the time it reminded me of a discussion I had had a few weeks before with Sujoy Srimal, then the general secretary of the Equitable Marketing Association in Calcutta. I had commented that some of the brushes being produced by a nearby cooperative seemed a bargain. 'No,' he said, 'they are not a bargain. They are cheap because the people are desperate to make a sale.' 'For us though,' I insisted, 'that means they are a bargain.' 'What a peculiar idea of a bargain you have in England,' Sujoy replied. 'For me, a bargain is an agreement where both parties are happy that they have got the best deal.' This conversation seemed to sum up how the marketplace should really function; not as cut-throat competition but as a mutual seeking of balance and joint satisfaction. One more element in what was becoming a distinctive view of business had emerged.

It is relatively easy to establish a new pattern of work in a new organization. At the beginning people are open to change and have often been attracted by the opportunity to try new directions. A spirit of innovation is frequently found in cooperatives and community businesses. Many of the people joining such organizations place a very high priority on the quality of the working relationships and being part of a structure in which they feel comfortable. Usually these organizations are fairly small and the idea that 'small is beautiful' takes on a particularly powerful significance for the members. As Traidcraft sought out other alternative businesses this emphasis on the small working group emerged as a common feature.

In Europe alternative trading was recruiting informed support more easily than in Britain, and it was here that problems about size had already been faced. Solidarisk Handel in Sweden had been founded in 1970 by a small group of young people who were concerned about the obstacles that capitalist nations had erected to prevent China participating easily in world trade. They had met with a good response, but found their very success threatening the cohesion of their group. After ten years they still retained the pattern of the early days. They had deliberately kept the turnover at the shop in Stockholm that was their main outlet at a constant level in spite of opportunities to expand.

In Britain I had long admired the development magazine *New Internationalist*. As I searched for new outlets for Traidcraft I got to know the small cooperative of about twelve people who wrote and published it. It was (and is) a group packed with ideas, talent and enthusiasm; why then, had they not expanded? They had been about the same size then for five years. Once again it had been a conscious decision to stay at a number where they could communicate directly with each other, both individually and in meetings. Their example led me to reflect on the experience of Tearcraft. I began to wonder whether the rapid growth and tensions with TEAR Fund had provided a cohesion amongst the staff that had got us past the level of fifteen to twenty-five jobs at which many organizations had chosen to consolidate. But what were the implications for Traidcraft? We had deliberately set out to achieve maximum growth and early after the launch of our second catalogue we could see that we were on course for a 250 per cent expansion in twelve months.

It seemed likely that, as a team of people, we would face two major internal problems if this rate of growth continued. First there would be that of coping with the pace of change. The initial group of seven who had moved from Tearcraft were involved in most aspects of the business in the first few months. We all helped unload a shipment, answer the phone, process orders, pack the goods, take the cheques to the bank, look after the stand at trade fairs, talk to voluntary reps and sweep the floor. But after twelve months jobs were becoming more specialized, and although the change suited some people who liked to concentrate on a particular area of work and develop particular skills there were others who regretted that their overall sense of being in touch with the business as a living organism was diminishing.

Second, my knowledge of organizations in which growth and constructive management had been relatively unplanned indicated that informal hierarchies of authority quickly established themselves to fill a managerial vacuum. In other words, if you do not visibly lead an organization, someone somewhere will be setting an agenda anyway. The direction that is given in this way can meet the immediate needs of the organization, but it becomes very hard to make such authority accountable. So not only did the jobs of individuals have to become 'narrower': the responsibilities of individuals and the paths of accountability had to be made clearer. To the observer it must have appeared that we were re-inventing the wheel. Any management textbook contained the structures that we were adopting and the techniques that we were using. Yet we spent hours working through these issues as a group, and the process of group discussion was to become a permanent feature of Traidcraft's management.

As we approached our second Christmas we needed to take on both permanent and temporary staff. We were still finding that notices posted in local churches were an effective way of recruiting, and as a result the majority of our candidates had a specific Christian commitment. In some respects their commitment created difficulties. People who would have had no particular views on how a secular company should be run had very definite ideas about how a *Christian* company should operate. Our open style of management also gave them an opportunity to express their views, and if you ask for people's opinions you have to listen when they give them. But most noticeably we seemed to be building up a staff who had more than their fair share of personal problems. In our small team, still less than twenty in November 1980, we had four people with serious mental or chronic physical illness, three individuals from broken or failing marriages, two university drop-outs and, just embarking on his secret career, a very determined thief.

I used to ponder over this with Brian and Jan, who had both

moved over from Tearcraft by then. 'Why is it that Christians seem to have so many problems?' pondered Brian. 'You'd think that they would have less. We seem to be turning into a social work department.' 'Come on, Brian,' said Jan. 'Think of the hours you spend counselling people yourself, both in and out of work. I think we have an atmosphere here where people don't feel threatened, where they can open up because they know they will find support.' I had mixed feelings about this response. As a fairly self-contained person I found it frustrating to see so much time being spent on dealing with personal issues and I recognized that I was useless at counselling. On the other hand I wanted the work environment to be supportive, to reflect concern for all the staff and to help people become more fulfilled. Fortunately there were many warm, outgoing people on the staff with a gift for encouraging others, and I was able to see my role as ensuring that they had space to operate as part of the Traidcraft 'culture'.

It was about this time that we began using the 'People before profit' slogan, and I suspect that we sometimes had our own staff in mind as well as the producers in the Third World. Now that our first year was over we were beginning to feel more comfortable about our ability to provide an ongoing service for those organizations that we had taken over from Tearcraft. Although Traidcraft was dependent on its suppliers I was only too aware of how dependent many people in developing countries were on our efforts to sell their work. One day I sat down to work out how directly the producer was benefitting. In our first financial year of eight months we sold goods mostly from the Jute Works in Bangladesh. They had received about £60,000 for these products, and, as their administrative costs were low, had paid about £55,000 to women in the producing cooperatives. After deducting the cost of the jute itself, which was bought by the women and of course provided an income for the farmer, only £48,000 remained. At that time the average income for a woman engaged part-time in handicraft work was about £45 a year. This incredibly small sum was nevertheless about two-thirds of the average wage for a man in Bangladesh and often made a critical difference in standard of living. The average family size was six persons and so, when my calculation was finished, I was amazed to find that our first year's work had contributed to a better life over twelve months for 6,400 people.

'There's no way we can publish these figures,' said Brian. 'They'll just give people a distorted idea of our effectiveness, and anyway £45 for a year's work sounds dreadful.' I agreed that it looked as if people were being grossly exploited, but remembered that the reality was very different. On a recent trip I had returned to one of the villages that I had first visited in 1974 whilst waiting for the relief flight to arrive. As I was negotiating the narrow path leading to the cluster of huts, slightly raised on a mound above the surrounding paddy fields, there was a torrential downpour. I had a waterproof, which I quickly put on, but the villagers with me were soaked. As we entered the village it looked depressingly the same. By this time I had learnt that the neat huts, the ponds with lilies and ducks and the waving palm trees of the countryside concealed a poverty far more desperate than the squalor of the cities. My hosts sat me down in an open hut and returned in dry clothes five minutes later bearing a cup of tea. I could not see what difference having an active handicraft cooperative had made.

'Well,' they said proudly, 'have you noticed all the changes over the past six years?' I said that my memory was not too good so perhaps they should point out them out. 'We're dry aren't we? Six years ago many people in this village would not have had a change of clothes, nor somewhere dry to keep them. Now we have many homes with tin roofs.' I noticed that corrugated iron had replaced some of the pest-harbouring thatch. 'Also we have built this community house that we are sitting in and your cup of tea comes with water from our new tube well. Didn't you wonder where the children are? Well, we can now afford for some of them to be sent to school, and when you are ready we want to show you our goats and our chickens and the new storage shed we have built.' And that was not all. They told me of plans to bring electricity to the village, of how a trader was thinking of opening a shop now there was a village where people had money and how he was trying to get the road improved so that his stock could be safely delivered. Nearly half the people could read and write, there was less sickness, and fewer people were having to go to Dhaka to find work.

I remember returning to Dhaka in a very positive frame of mind after that visit. The following day I went to an international trade fair that was being held on a site right in front of the Jute Works' office and warehouse. On leaving, right in front of the main entrance, I saw a small girl crouching down. She was begging with a tin can. Stretched in front of her was the body of an even younger boy. Now this was unusual even for Bangladesh. 'What is the matter?' I asked my Bangladeshi friend, who bent down and spoke to her. 'Her parents are dead, and now her brother has just died, she says she needs money to bury him, she knows no one else in the city. She is six years old.' I do not know what happened to this girl. We gave her money and left her begging. Normally I manage to blank out these sorts of incidents, which are still only too common, but this one has stayed with me because the girl was, at that time, the same age as my own daughter, and her dead brother was the same age as my son.

Incidents like these and the experience of evil and injustice can potentially undermine faith in a loving God. Why should there be suffering at all? If God exists is he perpetrating a vast swindle on us and laughing at our attempts to understand? Do we feel that somehow we, with our secure lives, are part of a sinister bargain, enjoying our happiness at the expense of others who live in misery? Is it one child or 40 million who will die each year from preventable causes? One destitute sleeping in a shop doorway or 500 million who will go to sleep tonight knowing the pangs of severe hunger? It makes no difference to those of us who believe in a God of love and justice, for the single case poses the same problem as 10 million. We must be able to answer; we must have a defence.

Not long after that visit to Bangladesh I went to Durham Cathedral with several other people from Traidcraft to hear Dom Helder Camara, then archbishop of Olinda and Recife in Brazil and one of the great champions of the poor in our time. Something he said stayed with me, puzzling me and encouraging me to understand why he said it and how it was relevant. In a slow, deliberate and deeply moving voice he said, 'We have to understand, there is no salvation without our brothers and sisters.' What did he mean? Is our salvation to be held ransom by the poor, even by those who reject God's love? I pondered about what salvation really was and came to understand that it was not primarily about being saved from the consequences of our sin, either in the form of punishment from others or internal guilt: salvation should not be thought of as being let off. Salvation is nothing unless it is the reality of breaking free from our sins themselves, having the possibility of total change and a new beginning. Then I began to understand how my 'brothers and sisters' came into the picture: their suffering also had to be redeemed and this was an action not only of God but a responsibility of all who claimed to love God.

I found my faith strengthened rather than weakened. How was it possible to drag some sort of meaning from this purpose-less suffering and death? Surely it could only be approached through the reality of God. And again I came to understand a little of how meaning could be found through an image that came to me of the person of Jesus. I saw him edging out along a vast balance arm of a set of weighing scales towards the poor, oppressed, and weak. It became increasingly dangerous for him, and he became more and more isolated. Then he reached the point of balance, the point of separation, of extreme suffering and aloneness, and he pressed on. By willingly taking into himself that unjust and meaningless suffering he allied himself with the suffering of the oppressed, of those who, like him, were experiencing powerlessness, injustice and death. And the balance changed, for in Jesus God affirmed that he is a God of justice and of love, and love demands that all injustices, great or small, be redeemed.

6

The Lifestyle Link

'Knick-knacks and luxuries, that's all you sell. I think that we would be able to consider more active support if you had products that were somewhat more functional.' I was listening to one of the senior executives of a major development agency. It was the beginning of 1981, and we had just had excellent Christmas sales. We needed to plan ahead so that the momentum could be maintained, and for some months I had been contacting church and development organizations to seek out ways of cooperation. My hope was that their supporters would be interested in Traidcraft's work.

I also felt strongly that we could offer many things in return. We had a new angle on practical development, we had a new approach to fund-raising by selling goods rather than asking for a donation that was likely to attract a wider public and, most of all, there were the products themselves. I had felt for a long time that the relationship between the development agencies and their casual supporters was very nebulous. Ideas and information were sent out by the agency, the donor sent a cheque or slipped some money in a tin: end of contact. Traidcraft was marketing products that literally brought a part of the Third World into the home through one of the ordinary mechanisms of everyday life, selling and buying. For most people the process of giving 'charity' is both unusual and uncomfortable. That is not to say that it is not important but at that time the average household was giving less than 80p a week to charity while spending more than £120 overall. I felt that it would be more effective to promote creative spending than charitable giving.

I had to recognize, however, that the comments about the range of Traidcraft products were largely true. Why else did we do 60 per cent of our business in the three months before Christmas if they were not for use as gifts? But I had some strong counter-arguments to support our position. 'First of all,' I explained to the head of overseas aid, 'we have to start with what the producers can actually make. Their skills are often traditional. If they learn new techniques their income drops during the learning period and often they are living hand to mouth. Also their culture is often worked into what they make.' At this point I thought of the community of stone craftsmen around Agra in India whose skills derived directly from those of the Persian artisans brought in centuries earlier to work on the Taj Mahal. 'Second, are you saying that there is no place for the gift, for the artefact that expresses someone's skill, sense of design and beauty? What sort of world would we have where everything was strictly functional?' I felt that the second remark was slightly below the belt. No one likes to be thought a Philistine even though the Traidcraft products could hardly be called high art. But I had saved the strongest point until last. 'Third, we are including functional things. What do you call wooden spoons, shopping bags, paint brushes, bookshelves and tea and coffee?' The reply was swift: 'But all this makes these producers dependent on you, and anyway, is the tea and coffee decaffeinated?' Clearly we still had some convincing to do with this particular agency. Nevertheless we were making converts elsewhere.

In our second catalogue we had begun to sell a tea that came from an estate in the south of Sri Lanka. I had been keen to expand beyond craft products in Tearcraft days and had come across this source then. The Waulugala estate was unusual in that it was owned by a trust set up by the Dissanayake family, the previous owners. The trust ran homes for orphaned and handicapped children, the elderly and the mentally ill. Half the profits from the tea estate went to the trust and the other half was divided between the tea workers in the form of a lump-sum annual bonus. In a good year the payment could be as much as the worker's total earnings for the same period.

I had not felt able to pursue this opportunity with Tearcraft as Mr Dissanayake was a devout Buddhist, but in 1979 I had visited the estate and arranged for Traidcraft to import the tea. The production of tea carried a long history of exploitation, much of it a colonial responsibility, and exploitive practices had not entirely ceased under the management of the major British tea companies. We had discussions with the World Development Movement, an organization campaigning for international development, about the possibility of marketing the tea under their name. The director of WDM, John Mitchell, was a member of the Traidcraft board and he was enthusiastic about the link up. In September 1980 we started selling 'WDM Tea. A high quality broken orange pekoe, 3 x 125g packets for £1.00'.

Not only was the producer the sort of community-based group that we wanted to support; in marketing our product under the name of WDM we were joining an existing campaign for justice in the trade of a major commodity. Average wages on the tea estates in India, Sri Lanka and East Africa, which supplied the vast majority of tea imports, were about 50p per day. The largest tea auction in the world was in London and the market was dominated by four major British companies. As a nation we drank 200 million cups of tea each day. There was no doubt that British-controlled companies were paying low wages to many estate workers and that conditions were poor. It was right to bring pressure on the major firms, but unless the consumer was prepared to pay more for the product, where was the money for the necessary improvements to come from?

With WDM tea, and later the range of other teas and teabags that Traidcraft developed, we were able to show that some people would pay a premium in order to give the producers a better deal. A few estates have improved conditions for their workers in response, but with Traidcraft's impact on the British tea market running at a fraction of a per cent, the need for much greater consumer support for action for justice was still apparent. Mounting a campaign and offering a reasonable alternative were essential steps but most critical of all was getting the ordinary member of the public committed to justice through trade.

We soon realized that dealing with tea was very different from importing handicrafts. We had entered the world of commodity trading, of futures, speculation, 'slippages' (shipments or quantities that mysteriously disappeared) and international politics. We had also moved into a business where high technical expertise was required. I had assumed that once we established our links in Sri Lanka the tea would be supplied without further difficulty. By a fortunate chance I had met a woman involved in importing Sri Lankan crafts to Britain whose husband was a partner in a large firm of tea brokers in Colombo. In this way I was initiated into the complexities of tea growing, buying, tasting and blending. I was able to arrange for the buying of the Waulugala tea at the Colombo auction and for it to be packed locally. The packing process added a surprising amount of extra value to the tea and created local jobs as well.

In the first year we sold the tea the comments about it ranged from 'the best I have ever tasted' to 'very poor quality'. We learnt that all major brands in Britain are blends, not only of teas from different countries but from different estates. They are often adjusted regionally to suit local water or taste preferences and for this reason they are all blended and packed in this country. Maintaining a consistent blend was a fine art and seasonal differences in teas from one estate would soon be noticeable to the discerning palate. Even a change in the curing process that took place on the estate could be spotted, as I realized when we had one very 'smoky' consignment. I later discovered that the hot-air drying flues in the Waulugala factory, which were supplied by a wood-burning furnace, had been leaking.

We began to look for other estates that met our buying criteria so that we could also blend, but in the meantime agreed to let the broker in Colombo mix in other teas to keep a consistent quality. The entire process had to be explained to our customers who must have become some of the most discriminating tea drinkers in the world.

WDM was passing 10 per cent of the final selling price back

to other development projects in Sri Lanka as well as supplying money to the Waulugala estate for improved housing. One of the groups being supported was seeking to help tea workers on other estates, mostly Tamils, by encouraging education and organization into unions. On my next visit to Colombo I was shown a newspaper story headlined 'British do-gooders fund Tigers'. The 'Tigers' were the Tamil Tigers, the main armed group fighting for an independent area in Sri Lanka for the minority Tamil population. Fortunately the names of WDM and ourselves had been so misquoted that they were unrecognizable, and the story had no long-term effect on our work; nevertheless it brought home to me the difficulty of drawing a line between issues of justice, politics and development.

Alongside the tea we had begun to sell instant coffee from Tanzania. Many of the same problems, from variable quality to political sensitivity, arose again. However many of our voluntary reps were delighted that we were moving into this area. Not only were tea and coffee products that could command regular sales, but they could also be used to illustrate some of the injustices of the world trading pattern. After a strong presentation from one of our reps in Kent on the evils of the international commodity trade and the connivance of big companies in exploiting the poor a member of the audience wrote and complained to his local MP. The protester was a senior employee of a multi-national food corporation, and in the reply that came back from the Minister of Overseas Development, Traidcraft was dismissed as 'well-meaning but naive'.

If I hoped we were well meaning I knew for certain that we were naive. We had to work hard at gaining the experience we needed to run a viable but altruistic business. It was not that things were going badly; indeed, we were beginning to demonstrate our independence. This was the time when our agreement with Tearcraft was coming to an end. We had bought our £60,000 worth of goods in the first year and taken over dealing with the groups they wanted to drop. Now, at the end of the second year, we had just received the last 25 per cent of the trade customers, who had been transferred on a gradual basis. We had been able to consolidate our good start and by the end of our third catalogue we had grown to be larger than Tearcraft. I must admit to feeling proud about our success.

My feelings highlighted for me one of the paradoxes involved in applying Christian values to the processes of business. Traidcraft had a set of objectives that would undoubtedly be to the benefit of the world's poor and underprivileged if they were fulfilled. Yet fulfilment involved successful operation on a large scale. The very pervasiveness of economic inequalities in our world meant than redressing the balance would require a massive transfer of resources. Achieving such a goal required a new economic and business approach that was more than a token: it required a system that would work on a large scale. To demonstrate the viability of such an approach we needed to enter the global marketplace. The problem was that to survive in this same marketplace we had to be efficient and competitive. It seemed we had to use those very tools of aggressive capitalism that had been partly responsible for the unequal distribution of wealth in the first place.

This dilemma was not unique to Traidcraft. It underlay a conference of Alternative Trading Organizations that took place at Amersfoort in Holland in 1981. The twenty-five groups that attended had many differences, but all were struggling with how to change the system whilst being part of it and using its mechanisms. It seemed that we all had our own approaches. GEPA from West Germany conducted the most thorough analysis of the groups from which it purchased and more than thirty types of criteria had to be met. Stichting Ideele Import from Holland traded only with 'socialist' countries, while Handelsfront in Sweden also demanded that those countries be 'anti-imperialist' towards their neighbours. Some groups dealt only in ethnic products unmodified by Western influence. Others felt that handicrafts were non-functional and perpetuated poverty so would only deal in food products. Most groups felt that marketing was a dirty word and that a clear stand had to be taken against the extravagant consumption patterns of the West, and yet all except one wanted to increase their turnover.

As always at conferences the real benefit came in exchanging information and making contacts on a one-to-one basis. It seemed that on issues of principle and procedure the alternative trade movement had little to hold it together except a desire for change. However we did agree to meet again in two years' time, with Traidcraft as the hosts. I returned home in a depressed mood. The groups that were seeking a new approach represented a tiny proportion amount of world trade, and yet we could not even agree amongst ourselves on a strategy for concerted action. The reality of day-to-day work and in particular the rapidly growing number of our voluntary representatives were a good antidote to the cosmic despair from which I suspect all workers in the field of social justice suffer occasionally.

The scheme that we had started in Tearcraft, which allowed individuals to sign up for extra information about the producers and discounts on the products, had been substantially developed over a period of six years. In 1979 many of the Tearcraft reps had also registered with Traidcraft and by 1982 this original core of 120 had grown to more than 400. We now had three people from Carliol Square working with this group by providing advice and support. A lot of our UK travel budget was spent on setting up weekend workshops around the country and visiting the reps in their own homes. No other ATO had a similar scheme and I had discussed it with a number of people at the Dutch conference.

'How can you afford to give them so much help?' was the usual comment. There was no doubt that the personal service we gave each rep was expensive. At that time we estimated that it cost us about £45 per rep per year. In addition to making visits we provided a monthly newsletter and a large range of subsidized educational and display materials. 'If we spent that sort of money on our supporters,' said Dieter Hartmann, a colleague from Dritte Welt Laden in West Germany, 'we'd be out of business in a few months.'

The answer was a simple one: commitment. The average rep was not only spending five or six hours a week planning and running Traidcraft activities, but also had £300 worth of products that had to be stored in cupboards, spare bedrooms and garages. Reps had taken on short-let shops at Christmas, shivered at hired market stalls in the winter, stood in the rain at agricultural shows, fitted out caravans as mobile displays, visited schools, offices and factories and lobbied local council meetings. As a result of these sorts of activities the average sales of a rep in 1982 came to £700.

A development agency thinks long and hard about its contact with supporters. A general mailing may result in, at best, a 10 per cent response, but there is the risk of making the donors think that their money is just being used to produce more pieces of paper and employ more Post Office staff. The Traidcraft reps had a different relationship. They were not only doing a job of work in which they needed skilled support and encouragement: they were also our customers and we owed them good service. In some ways the relationship mirrored that of Traidcraft with its producers in the Third World. We were mutually dependent on each other, and only concern for each others' needs would make the partnership work.

One of our most active reps had been involved since the earliest days. I first met Sheila Mutler on a very wet morning in May 1975. It was at one of her twice-yearly second-hand clothes sales organized around her church in the small town of Paddock Wood in Kent. Sheila had been sending the proceeds from these sales to TEAR Fund and she thought that there might an interest in the products from Bangladesh, so I arrived with a van full of jute. In the evening we compared notes. 'It's my best ever,' said Sheila. '£550 in cash and still a lot of stock left. How did you get on?' I had not been so successful and had taken £35 in total. Sheila was righteously angry. 'They know so little around here,' she said. 'Most folk couldn't point out where Bangladesh is let alone recognize the need for dignified trade.'

Sheila, like many of our reps, was filled with a real passion for justice, which I found inspiring each time we talked. She had a gift for direct speaking whether it was to the Mother's Union in the church hall in the afternoon or the Labour Party in a Tonbridge pub in the evening. When Jan decided to put together a handbook for the reps she asked Sheila to write the section on public speaking. 'You asked me to speak at a big meeting about the Brandt Report,' Sheila recalled as we discussed the reps scheme. 'You know that I left school before

I was fifteen and I was scared stiff because so many of the people there had real intellectual calibre. Well, I got the book and made thirty-eight pages of notes, which I condensed to twelve. Then I got Hansard and read through the debate in Parliament about it and only after that did I begin to feel a little bit of confidence.

'I could spend my whole life trying to get something through to people. Do you know, I was speaking to an early retirement club the other day and one of the blokes said, "They'd be all right in the Third World if they didn't spend so much money on arms." So I asked him, "Who do you think is the second biggest supplier of arms in the world? It's us. We're selling them the stuff to help our balance of payments. Don't you think that's sick?"'

Sheila saw that selling actual products provided tangible evidence of the need for justice in trade. Particularly in affluent Kent she frequently came across people who used corruption or laziness in the Third World or inefficiency by the development agencies as excuses for not helping. 'The fact that you can put products before them that are the result of someone's work and offer them at a fair price really knocks the ground from under their feet.' Many of the reps found the same and some had spectacular success with innovative methods of selling. One couple in Leeds bought one of every product in the catalogue and mounted a display of the goods in their home. They asked all their friends round in the course of a fortnight and sold goods worth £3,000.

I once asked Sheila where her concern and commitment had come from. 'Two things, I think,' she said. 'My father was an active trade unionist and so working for justice and basic rights for people seemed to run in the family. Also I'd not gone to church much until we came to Paddock Wood and the idea of helping the poor that people had there was through Christian Aid. I thought, "All they're doing is collecting from everyone in the village; this isn't *Christian* Aid, its *Everybody* Aid." And so that made me think about what Christians should really be doing to help, and you know the rest.'

The same feelings were expressed by a rep from Scotland. 'For so many of us the chief thing is that you have enabled *us* to make a contribution and to *do* something instead of just feeling guilty and appalled. I am afraid that I am really very small beer as far as reps go, but even so I keep on, encouraged by the information and support from Traidcraft. One thing that I am grateful for is the range of prices — this is a former mining and textile area near Kilmarnock and it is still very depressed. I find that at the local gala day or cattle show people are interested in the origins of the goods but haven't a lot of money to spend. Selling foodstuffs is a good idea when people don't have a lot of extra money. For too long I have been appalled by the philosophy that treats acquisitiveness as a virtue, without doing anything more than view the whole sorry business with disdain. I want to wake up and become part of a movement of creative consumers meeting the acquisitive/aggressive society "head on". Thank you for your professional and informed approach to alternative trading.'

By the end of 1988 more than 2,500 people had been Traidcraft reps, with 1,500 of those still active and selling in total more than £1.5 million a year. The average 'life' of a rep seemed to be about four years although there were still more than fifty that had given nearly ten years' service. Dozens of reps had visited producer groups and experienced ordinary life in the Third World at first hand. Hundreds of them had appeared in their local press, on local radio stations or on regional television programmes, and most were established on the lists of visiting speakers or activity organizers for a host of clubs, associations and community groups.

Certainly by 1982 the reps scheme had already emerged as one of the most successful elements of Traidcraft's work. Its popularity was partly due to the fact that it offered people an opportunity for action using contacts and skills that they already possessed. But as we developed materials for the reps to use it was brought home to me yet again how great was the gulf between rich and poor. Traidcraft, at best, was one of the plants of hope struggling to survive in a barren landscape. What else could be done?

I had a talk with Brian about this feeling and mentioned that perhaps, now that Traidcraft seemed to be well on its feet, I should be moving on, looking for a fresh approach and a new initiative. The strength of his reaction surprised me. 'You can't leave now,' he said, 'we're only just beginning and people will think you're jumping from one thing to another without any real commitment.' I valued his advice, but although I decided that I should stay with Traidcraft it didn't stop me setting down some ideas for a broader concept. It was a complex proposal and this first attempt to define it was largely intuitive, mainly unresearched and therefore very over-simplified. I set it down, largely for my own benefit, in a 'Beyond Traidcraft' paper that I never circulated.

The main idea was that public support for a more just world needs to be mobilized in a new way. It needed to be through the ordinary activities of life: through work, through buying goods to meet everyday requirements, through saving and even through leisure. It needed to be on a huge scale to have any effect and it needed to be politically realistic. The main point would, however, be to transfer resources from the First World to the Third.

Many developing countries are too poor to be able to produce or purchase the materials, equipment or skills that they need either to establish or to maintain a pattern of growth that will enable their people to have even the basic necessities. Differing forms of assistance to all these countries transfers some resources from the rich nations, but often it is in the form of tied aid. Dumped grain surpluses, arms sales, expensive high-tech or capital-intensive projects have rightly given a bad name to assistance that is linked to the donor's own requirements or political agenda. At the other end of the spectrum there is the provision by autonomous development agencies of specific technical assistance in the form of personnel, consultancy, or, infrequently, equipment. It is the case that many agencies see the provision of grant-aid to a partner project as essentially the 'cleanest' form of assistance as it allows maximum discretion to the recipient within an agreed project.

As development agencies become more sophisticated in their fund raising they increasingly recognize that they are essentially in the marketing business. People who make a donation are buying the 'package of satisfactions' that is attached to any product. The satisfactions may not be as tangible as those attached to a new car, a holiday in Crete or a new fitted kitchen, but they exist and are the real motivators.

The new approach that I was working towards introduced another powerful motivator into the aid process: a well-defined element of sacrificial support for a more sustainable economy and lifestyle at home, linked with a benefit that could be seen to be applied on behalf of the poor. In other words, people needed to be drawn to the idea of keeping their lifestyle within modest bounds so that they could meet their own needs and have enough over to share with the poorer nations. In addition the system served to highlight areas of interdependency and also awareness of implications of lifestyle and expenditure. These were distinct advantages that conventional fund-raising did not normally have.

The system was intended to combine direct government support, industrial sponsorship (both commercial and via the unions), and local government and government agency participation, but would draw the bulk of its funding from individual participation. It was a scheme that had the potential to operate at a level comparable with the largest transnational organization and that could also provide the necessary element of personal involvement to maintain interest and enthusiasm. This was my pipe-dream and it was perhaps no more than whistling in the dark, but I tried to work out some examples of what I was reaching towards. I toyed with the following example.

The frequency with which people change their cars in the UK is not solely determined by economic efficiency. Allow that the average saving to the individual of retaining a car one year more than would normally be the case can be calculated at £400, having adjusted for additional maintenance, depreciation and the like. The non-economic cost is a marginally higher risk of breakdown and a lower satisfaction in driving an older model.

If 10 per cent of all the personal owners of cars in this country could be encouraged to take this step each year then, assuming that half of their purchases are imports anyway, there would be a net reduction of 5 per cent in that category of vehicles sold, which would certainly have a major effect on employment within the car industry. The £20 million saved by the individuals concerned, if diverted directly in the form of grant aid to overseas development projects, would certainly cause hardship to those made redundant in the motor industry as a result of lower sales. If, however, this money was spent on appropriate vehicles for export to the Third World at minimal cost then employment would be maintained in Britain and probably increased due to the reduction in imports.

Individuals, therefore, would be encouraged to sign up for what would effectively be a period of self-denial linked to a particular aspect of their lives. The money would be nominally earmarked for a parallel development category and the donor would receive support material, say quarterly, on the progress of various projects within this category.

Cars feature in this illustration, but there would be many categories in the scheme and the individual could choose to take up more than one. Possible sectors were household appliances, entertainment equipment, kitchen and bathroom refittings, holidays, food, drink and cosmetics: there really was an endless list. The key point was the link between adjusting one's lifestyle and helping the poor.

The organizing body for this scheme would need to tap into substantial funds in order to operate on a large scale. At that time the ethical investment movement was getting under way in America, and I wondered whether some type of altruistic financial institution might be established here in Britain. In fact the following year, when we were seeking to raise money for Traidcraft, we had discussions with the Bank of England on this very issue. But there was also another way that this scheme could be linked to industry and employment.

For some years an organization called Tools for Self-Reliance had been refurbishing donated hand tools for export to communities in the Third World. My idea was to take the concept and apply it to various types of light and medium industrial equipment that would be appropriate for subsidized export to countries that did not have the facilities to produce such plant themselves. Renovation and testing could be done in factories that were provided, sponsored and staffed through a contribution from private industry, a union or government and organized by the resource transfer corporation. Some refurbishment would need to be done on contract by original manufacturers or by specialists. The range of equipment would be vast, ranging from sewing machines and printing presses through machine tools and agricultural machinery to cranes and canning factories.

The funds generated by the 'lifestyle-link' scheme could be channelled into the industrial refurbishment programme to some extent. The whole concept would be operable on a massive scale and could be applied to any Western industrial country in order to benefit a developing country with a low level of industrial infrastructure. In the longer term the Third World would become less dependent upon the First through this process. The result would be fewer exports, more imports and the gradual coming together of rich and poor economies — something that can only happen in any event if the rich reduce their consumption and aim for a more sustainable way of living.

As I was thinking through some of these concepts I was aware that I was dreaming dreams, but where was the line that divided the dream from the vision and the vision from the reality? I realized that I needed the vision, the dream, as an antidote to the apparent hopelessness of the global picture of greed and despair. But it had to be more than an illusion: it had to be realizable. It might be a fiction but it was science fiction not fantasy, and this vision was not just a personal matter.

Through Traidcraft I was coming to see that one of the things that a radical organization requires is a blend of visionary and practical ideas. The time-honoured phrase of the evangelist calling for converts in a congregation, 'I want you to get up out of your seat' expresses this well. Once the step towards action has been taken, individuals will be much more open to receiving additional information to support and consolidate the experience that they have just had. A few years ago researchers discovered an interesting fact. The people who paid most attention to advertisements for major consumer products such as cars or washing machines were those who had just bought the product being advertised. It was apparently the case that they were seeking reassurance, looking for confirmation of the rightness of their purchase. Any well-trained salesperson knows that satisfied new owners are the best advocates for a product as they seek to convince others of their good judgment. The conclusion is that if you can get individuals to act then their commitment increases substantially.

Traidcraft was providing that first step: the opportunity to purchase. Anyone could take this option, and it was an action that most people perform several times a day. From that point a number of other options were offered, some perhaps requiring a little more involvement than the person was prepared to give at that moment but nevertheless available when the time came. Welding all these potential actions together was the overall vision or objective. It would be a vision set out in such a way that individuals would know that they were not alone, that they were acting with others, that the scheme was so big that it could accommodate many different views and perspectives and yet provide a rallying point. Every four or five years we have the opportunity to vote for a new government in Britain. Every day we vote with the way we spend our money. Gradually the idea of the power of consumer politics was taking shape in my own thoughts about Traidcraft's future.

So this was the context in which I dreamed the dreams, and I was not dreaming alone. Traidcraft's customers were still predominantly drawn from a Christian base and ideas drawn from liberation theology were filtering into Christian thinking. Dietrich Bonhoeffer had said as far back as 1932, 'There is no theological reflection in isolation from community. The isolation of the individual is the basic error of Protestant theology.' This renewed emphasis on theology coming from the experience of the community underpinned the ideas that were coming from South America and which are still making their way, not without difficulty, into the churches of the Western world today.

According to Leonardo Boff, a leading figure in liberation theology, this type of thinking starts with those who are suffering. It is based on 'a prophetic and comradely commitment to the life, cause, and struggle of these millions of debased and marginalized human beings, a commitment to ending this historical-social iniquity'. Of course we all suffer, but it would be patronizing and evasive to compare our life opportunities with those of the Indian peasant or the slum-dweller in Mexico City. So it is particularly important to listen to the emphasis of a leading liberation theologian like Gustavo Gutierrez when he says that we should begin, not with theology itself, nor even with the Bible, but with our place in the world and what we can do to work for justice.

For me it had been the impact of a suffering world, an impact that somehow came through the unreal years of student life, that made me seek ways in which the power of business could be placed at the service of the poor rather than used as a mechanism to exploit them. Over fifteen years I have had the privilege of travelling widely, visiting many countries, and working with many people who are committed to the service of the poor and many others who are poor. However, the relevance of liberation theology can be found closer to home.

A friend of mine is a vicar with a parish in Salford, Greater Manchester. It seems to have almost every social problem except gross materialism within its boundaries. 'How are things going, Geoff?' I asked on the phone one day. 'Very well,' he replied. 'The congregation is still growing slowly; it's up to about sixty now. Most of them have serious problems: you know, abuse, debt, unemployment, severe mental disorders, problems about sexual identity.' He said this in such a positive way that I commented, 'You seem almost pleased about it.' ' I am,' he replied. 'Look, I was talking to a colleague last week who has three hundred coming regularly to his church and he was telling me that he knew of no serious problems at all amongst them. That made me quite concerned. My view is that the church should be a place where we can open up and share our difficulties. I would be worried if I wasn't let in on people's suffering.'

Salford and São Paulo are closer to each other than they are to Surbiton, but the creative and spiritually regenerative ideas that they are producing have to be given the opportunity to enrich our arid materialism. Traidcraft was beginning to provide a channel along which those ideas could travel carried by the life-blood of the enterprise system itself, namely the flow of products. Those of us who are not poor ourselves are thereby cut off from the poor, no matter how deep our compassion. But being moved is not enough. We need to exercise an option to help the poor, to take a practical step.

I think it was this practical side of our work that was beginning to convince some of the development agencies that Traidcraft was able to provide a new approach for both supporters and recipients alike. Thanks to Charles Elliott, then director of Christian Aid, and Martin Bax, the associate director, the 1983/84 catalogue went out in a special version to more than sixty thousand supporters of Britain's largest Christian development agency. It was the start of a partnership that has been immensely supportive for Traidcraft and that has had the effect of helping to keep the company abreast of current thinking and action in development practice.

7

Food for Thought

In December 1982 one of our reps sent us a parcel containing a Christmas cake. The accompanying letter explained that it was made entirely with products supplied by Traidcraft. The rather heavy consistency was due to the fact that ground brown rice and cracked wheat were not an exact substitute for flour, although the honey that replaced the sugar made a very pleasant contribution.

During that year we had decided to introduce a range of wholefoods. Deciding to launch into this new product range had not been at all straightforward as most of the foods did not come from groups that met our normal purchasing criteria; indeed, in most cases, we only knew the country of origin. On top of this problem was the very sensitive issue of selling food from the Third World where hunger was endemic. I had argued energetically that we should be moving into areas that gave us the opportunity to campaign about trading inequities and that also linked up with related lifestyle issues. In this case it was the need to promote a healthy diet in Britain and the West, which would in turn encourage the traditional agriculture of developing countries.

Our three years' experience in importing tea and coffee had shown us a little of the massive power of the international food industry. The main commodities were traded in quantities of thousands of tonnes, and often the scale and costs of processing and packing made it very difficult for a small company to enter the market. The Agrofax experience had shown me that is was possible to carve out a niche for a particular product, but also warned of the dangers of enthusiastic amateurism. Our policy, evolved over several years, was to provide poor farmers and agricultural workers in the Third World with an alternative outlet for their foods. We aimed to buy from community-based groups of farmers, countries seeking justice for their rural poor through active development policies and groups who processed and packed locally-grown foods.

We developed part of the range in conjunction with Community Foods in London, a company that was run by a group of Christians. It was committed to promoting wholefoods and had become the largest importer servicing the growing network of local wholefood cooperatives and shops. To start with we offered a 'Food for Thought' pack, a specially designed display and presentation box filled with twenty-five types of wholefoods, a recipe book, a traditional Bangladeshi paddy winnower and a rice spoon from Bangladesh. A dozen different leaflets dealing with nutrition, agricultural reform, land use and other food-related topics completed a package that we hoped would enable any individual or organization to mount a professional display on the causes of world hunger.

The quantities in which food had to be purchased meant that before we could start to contract for container loads of any product we needed some assurance that we would have the customers who would buy it. But how to get the customers without offering the product? We broke the vicious circle with a compromise, initially buying food products through Community Foods where our only information was that they came from the Third World. We established a policy in which we gave ourselves three years to make significant progress towards identifying and dealing with specific food-producing groups. We felt that this approach would give us enough time to build up regular sales outlets, which would then enable us to deal directly with overseas producers for bulk orders. Brown sugar was a commodity for which this strategy worked well in practice.

We had been importing craft products from a group set up to provide work for handicapped young people in Mauritius, but the range had never been particularly successful. I noticed that our local supermarket had begun to sell at a very reasonable price brown sugar that was produced in Mauritius but packed in the UK. I contacted Paul Draper, a friend from Tearcraft days who had set up the craft group, and asked him if his people could establish a small packing operation on the island. Paul reported that all the sugar was sold through the Mauritius Sugar Syndicate who were not unsympathetic but who insisted that their minimum quantity for sale was 224 tonnes. A quick calculation showed that such a purchase represented 448,000 bags of sugar, far more than we could hope to sell at the time. We had to rethink.

I contacted Billington's, the company that was importing and packing the sugar in the UK. Would it do an 'own label' for us? It would, but the minimum order was 50 tonnes. That quantity was a lot less than 224 tonnes and did not seem an unrealistic amount for us to sell. We decided to go ahead. After a few months the sales figures were sufficiently good that I again rang Paul. 'I think we will be able to go ahead with the sugar packing idea after all,' I told him. 'But it will probably take us two years to sell the first shipment.' We talked around the idea a little more and, without too much persuasion, I agreed to Paul's suggestion to visit Mauritius to help plan the scheme and to talk to the Sugar Syndicate.

By that time, in late 1983, I had ceased to do a great deal of travelling as others had taken on the specialized work of product development and liaison with the producer groups. I had never enjoyed the experience of travel as some people do, always finding that I became homesick after a couple of weeks. We had also established a tradition on our overseas visits of staying in basic accommodation and making every hour count, so each trip tended to be very hard work. I must admit, however, that the idea of a visit to a noted holiday island had some appeal. Mauritius has a population of only one million and, with an average income per head of about £1000, is by no means one of the poorest countries in the world. But there is still much in the way of basic development that needs to take place.

What struck me most, however, was not the beaches but the people. Mauritius is an island that had no inhabitants at all until the seventeenth century; today its population consists of ethnic groups from Asia, Africa and Europe who live together in an atmosphere of openness and harmony. The beaches also lived up to their reputation, but the day I had earmarked to explore them coincided with the start of tropical storm Celeste and 100 mph winds. It was not the tourist season.

The main resources were the climate and the land. The island's landscape had a well-ordered appearance. Tea gardens and fields of sugar cane covered most of the cultivated land and the production of these crops was the major source of employment. Britain had obtained 95 per cent of its sugar from the colonies in the days of the Empire, but since the early 1970s a major change had taken place. Thanks to EEC subsidies European farmers now produced a huge surplus of beet sugar that was dumped on the world market at a massive loss. At the time I was in Mauritius the world market price for sugar was £103 a tonne. The EEC were paying about £270 a tonne. Although this was bad news for most of the Third World it was a windfall for Mauritius. Former colonial countries had been able to negotiate special quotas that the European Community would buy at the subsidized rate. Mauritius had done especially well with its quota, perhaps because families of French descent owned many estates, perhaps because it had rotated as a colony of Holland, France, and Britain, and perhaps because so many German tourists went there for their holidays.

Although 500,000 tonnes of refined sugar was sold to Europe none of it was packed on the island. One of the attractions for Traidcraft about most forms of food was the packaging. Not only could the value of the product to the suppliers be increased, but also the pack could carry well-presented educational and campaigning information. Our 'own label' packs from Billington's had featured points about the EEC sugar subsidies, and to this we would now be able to add the fact that packing in Mauritius increased value of the sugar to the suppliers by 40 per cent and created useful jobs.

The plan was to buy both sugar and tea in bulk and pack it into 500g and 125g packs respectively. The graphics department at Traidcraft was drawing up the artwork for the pack, but we needed to find package makers and printers in Mauritius. As in most developing countries there were numerous small businesses prepared to undertake jobbing work that would have been the province of the large, specialist firm in the UK. We found box and carton makers, a printer who would print on the packaging film we needed, a supplier of paper for the inner liner of the tea boxes and a sheet metal worker who would fabricate hoppers and funnels. Traidcraft shipped out two high-accuracy hand-held weighing balances and two heat sealers. At last Craft Aid, Mauritius, was in business in time for the forthcoming catalogue.

Any readers who have set up their own business will be saying 'I bet it didn't really happen like that' and of course they will be right. Over six months all sorts of things went wrong, but enough went right to get the end result. We needed to compromise on many issues, knowingly settle for second best and make several mental notes that we would set this or that right next time around. But we were in business with a combined product and message that was new to the British public, and soon Craft Aid had a further order from Dritte Welt Laden in Germany. The establishment of the sugar-packaging facility had involved the very simplest technology, but it had only been possible because Traidcraft had poked its nose into all sorts of activities during the course of its development.

A few months later, in May 1983, we were hosting the bi-annual conference of Alternative Trading Organizations, and many of the visiting organizations were puzzled by Traidcraft's large number of staff. For every £5 worth of goods we sold we spent £1 on salaries whereas most of our sister organizations in Europe and America, including Oxfam Trading which most closely resembled Traidcraft, sold £8-9 worth of products for each £1 of salary. The reason for this difference was that Traidcraft retained control of many activities that others contracted out. We had our own photographic studio, our own printing and graphics department and eventually did our own typesetting as well. We had always rented older premises in need of renovation and repair so we had our own maintenance team. We had established our own packaging facilities, first for instant coffee and then for many other food products that could not be packed in the country of origin. As time went on we wrote our own computer software, manufactured a wide range of recycled stationery, developed new product ranges, worked out job evaluation and appraisal systems, put together a more 'ethical' investment package for our pensions and even launched our own share issue without sponsorship or underwriting.

Undoubtedly we suffered from a lack of professionalism in most of these activities. We re-invented the wheel several times and made obvious and avoidable mistakes. Against these disadvantages there were normally substantial cost savings and the accumulation of skills and experience within the team. However, it was something more intangible that I felt was our most important gain: we were affirming our identity as an alternative company, we were saying, 'It *can* be done another way' and we were building up our own confidence in preparation for doing the really big things.

As a result of these varied activities we felt able to consider fairly complex undertakings with our partner groups in the Third World. In most cases we had already been through many of the difficulties that they would face as their businesses grew, both technical and managerial. In some cases our knowledge of the problems probably made us over-sympathetic to our partners when they did not meet delivery or quality requirements. Getting the right balance between the hard, driving pressure of commercial competition and support for a well-meaning partner struggling to create jobs for the disadvantaged is a daily consideration for every alternative trading group.

Early 1983 had seen us celebrate our first £1 million of sales in a year, an occasion that called for cream cakes at morning coffee break. Ray Skinner, chairman of the board since 1979, with a memory supplemented by a daily diary, was able to recall that he had asked me, as Traidcraft opened in August 1979, how long it would be before we made a million. I had apparently estimated five years. Clearly I had not allowed for the vitality that Traidcraft was displaying, a vitality that was to bring even more far-reaching changes during the following twelve months.

From our top-floor base in our Carliol Square warehouse we had now spread onto four other floors and across into two adjacent buildings. We had five separate storage, packing and office areas connected by narrow stairwells and three service lifts that had recently celebrated their fiftieth birthday. About 25,000 square feet of space housed £500,000 of bulky stock and a staff of forty-five people. As we reviewed the year ahead we realized that we would need at least another 10,000 square feet to cope with the planned 45 per cent increase in turnover. However, no more floors of the warehouse complex seemed likely to come onto the market. That was why March 1983 saw Jan, Brian, Bob Foreman and I gazing at the limitless expanse of a 58,000 square foot warehouse.

The four of us had driven to the Team Valley Trading Estate, which lay about two miles to the west of Carliol Square on the other side of the Tyne. Team Valley had been the first government industrial estate in the country, opened somewhat belatedly in 1936 to help deal with the economic slump after the 1929 stock market crash. At its peak it had employed more than 25,000 people and was still physically the largest in the country, although now with only a third of that workforce. There were, consequently, a lot of empty buildings: solid, functional factory blocks put up in the late 1940s and early 1950s. It was one of these properties that we were now looking at.

Unit 123 had been built as a carton-making plant and was equipped to handle heavy bales of paper. There were still the railway tracks leading up to the back door, although the spur to the main east coast line had long since been converted to a dual carriageway. Inside were two massive gantry cranes running at right angles to each other, 300 feet across the building and 150 feet down it. There were also pigeons, starlings and sparrows, which had found their way in through the broken roof lights. In the office block at the front of the warehouse we found a notable collection

of fungi. There were signs of damp and dilapidation everywhere.

In spite of its condition the advantages were enormous. The
ample space was all on one level and there were big loading bays
and parking facilities. The other main advantage was the price:
£103,000 for a 125-year lease on the building and a further one-
and-a-half acres of attached land. A new factory that size would
have cost over £1 million in the North-East, at least double that
in the South. We decided to recommend to the board that if we
could get a mortgage we should go ahead, although we would
have to spend another £150,000 to get the place in reasonable
condition.

Team Valley was an ideal spot for a business. As the South-
East became more and more congested and expensive it became
clear that inertia and personal prejudice played a large part in
a company's choice to relocate. Even employees on the lowest
wage levels at Traidcraft could afford to buy their own home,
something that was impossible for our counterparts in development agencies in the South even on much higher salaries. Very
few people had more than a thirty minute journey to work and
many could reach the premises within ten minutes. We had some
of Britain's most beautiful countryside surrounding us; even the
estate had attractively wooded slopes to the west. Just over the
river in Newcastle was the country's best regional shopping
centre and Tyneside had a vast range of arts and entertain-
ments. Additionally, the area was one where local authorities
took seriously the needs of the less privileged in society and
did something about them.

Help in buying the building came from an unexpected
source. The European Coal and Steel Community offered us
an attractive loan as we were in an area where major closures
in those industries had taken place. Their offer was made on
the condition that our jobs were open to redundant miners or
steel workers. It was with few regrets that we began the process
of moving from our above-ground warren in Carliol Square. By
September 1983 we had all made the transfer, leaving behind
only our shop, which benefitted from staying close to the city
centre. For the first time in four years I had an office that had

natural light. The main misgiving that I heard expressed was that much of the excitement had now disappeared from the lunchtime cricket matches. In Carliol Square the pitch was on the roof of the five-storey building and trying to save a boundary was slightly hazardous.

The pioneering spirit came out again as we advanced steadily into the remoter areas of the building, reclaiming them for productive purposes. The gantry cranes unfortunately had to be sold for scrap. The former director's suite became the computer room, and in the main warehouse we faced the problem of creating working spaces that were moderately warm in the winter. The task was not an easy one, and the first frosts led to a bulk purchase of company-issue body warmers. The new boiler room doubled up as the only area where smoking was allowed, the heat being some compensation for the otherwise spartan conditions. When fewer than 15 per cent of the staff smoke then those that do can expect little in the way of opportunity to indulge themselves.

Our move coincided with our developing approach to training and equipping the people in the company with new skills. We were aware that the the sixty or so people working with Traidcraft at that time had an average age of about thirty; few had professional or business qualifications, and not many had commercial working experience either. The attitude that the workforce of a company is a cost rather than a resource is still common and often leads to short-sighted decisions being made in times of crisis. However, Traidcraft was rapidly expanding and we committed ourselves to a substantial programme of training and staff development. Many staff went on the excellent local courses available, both technical and academic, and participated in the programmes run by the Industrial Society, which were often tailored to their own particular needs.

Alongside these business-oriented courses we supported staff in programmes that looked at issues such as self-assertiveness, group relationships and counselling. Work can play an important part in a person's own development as an individual. Just as training was needed to help people cope with new technical responsibilities in their jobs, support was also necessary in the more personal aspects of management and coping with change.

I realized that I was the chief executive of a company that was becoming more complex by the month and was conscious that I had never had any formal management training: all my learning had been done on the job. Although I still felt that studying sociology and theology provided the best grounding for a business career and that setting up a small business provided the best experience, I was aware of an accumulating weight of background knowledge. It was beginning to feel as if I had thrown years of paperwork into a large filing cabinet and not had time to sort it out. I wondered if there was anything that might help Traidcraft get better value out of the fourteen years' worth of jumble inside my head.

After checking with the University of Newcastle I found that a part-time course offering a master's degree in business administration (MBA) had been running for two years. At first I was daunted by the prospectus. The amount of work required was substantial, demanding about twenty hours a week over three years. I would have to fit my studying into my spare time. During the course I might come to understand the basics of financial accounting, explore the mysteries of organizational behaviour or learn the correct process for plant layout. On the other hand I might reach a state of despair trying to cope with statistics, macro-economics or labour relations. My colleagues, encouraged by the fact that I would be out of the office one day a week, encouraged me to apply.

I suppose it will sound irresponsible if I say that once the course work began I felt very much like a boy let loose in a timber yard with a new carpentry kit. The average age of my fellow students was about thirty-five and we came mostly from business, although we also had a social services director, a prison governor and an army major. Many of my colleagues on the course had little freedom to apply the theoretical management tools that we were learning about, but I did not suffer from this problem. Week after week at our Wednesday planning meetings my fellow senior managers at Traidcraft would groan, often audibly, as I rolled out yet another set of ideas from the lectures on operational management or business policy.

You win some and you lose some. Our early schemes involving 'Management by Objectives' were not a resounding success. On the other hand we did begin to equip ourselves with a long-term strategy for the company and revised it annually in a written strategic plan. We came to analyze our strengths and weaknesses, see the opportunities and recognize the threats. It turned out to be a particular advantage for us that my course stressed the importance of business policy, for as Traidcraft grew it became more important that the company understood what it was and where it was going. I ended up doing my final year dissertation on 'Corporate Strategy in Alternative Trading Organizations' and as I began to write it I still firmly believed that Traidcraft was somehow special because of what it was doing.

As I struggled to make the theory apply to the case in point, a pre-requisite in any piece of work short of a PhD thesis, I began to discover that all the distinctive activities of the company had been paralleled in other places and at other times. It was a process similar to that which the New Testament scholar goes through in finding out that the component ideas about God and humanity that Jesus expressed can all be found dotted here and there through other Jewish writings of the time. I talked over this commercial 'crisis of faith' with Paul Miller, the senior lecturer in the Department of Industrial Management.

'What are you so surprised about?' asked Paul. 'Of course Traidcraft is using conventional business and management techniques. It's not the systems you're using, it's *how* you're using them that makes Traidcraft unique. I noticed something quite different about your organization as an operating company when I visited you the other day. Has anyone else told you that?' Yes, I told him, they had. We had just been presented with the results of a financial strategy survey conducted by a major finance institution as part of a government programme to encourage small businesses. The consultants had made exactly the same comment.

A few months later I was talking to a new member of staff

and got a very similar view. Gordon had been made redundant as a supervisor when a local British Steel rolling mill closed. 'If they asked me back now I wouldn't go,' he said, 'even though the salary here is much less. The atmosphere is fantastic, stress and pressure are much less and there's a lot of job satisfaction.' Traidcraft was not a perfect company to work for, but there was something over and above the 'going-places, pulling-together' feeling that should be present in any organization. I cannot define it other than through the paradox of saying that Traidcraft was a company with double standards. We wanted to use the best management techniques and to be efficient, profitable, creative and caring. We also wanted to hold these standards up to another set of values — ones that the majority of people in the company derived from their personal faith.

We tried to define this intangible quality of Traidcraft when all the staff worked on setting out a statement of Traidcraft's objectives. Over several months a document emerged that probably said as much about strategy and methods as objectives, but it did reflect the attempt that was always going on in the company to break down the division between the spiritual and the secular.

TRAIDCRAFT'S OBJECTIVES

Traidcraft, following an extended discussion and consultation period with staff, shareholders, customers and representatives of partner production groups, sets down the following objectives as defining the main purposes of Traidcraft plc as it works in collaboration with the Traidcraft Exchange. These objectives should not be regarded as a mould within which all future developments take place but rather as a framework enabling a steady and purposeful growth. A regular review every two years by the trustees of the Traidcraft Exchange and the directors of the company in consultation with those groups mentioned above will seek to ensure that Traidcraft tests its experience acquired in practical action for justice in trade against these objectives in a continuing process.

Traidcraft aims to establish its own more equitable trading system that will express the principles of love and justice fundamental to the Christian faith. Practical service and a partnership for change will characterize the organization, which puts people before profit.

Just Trade = Fairer Systems

Traidcraft will aim to contribute to the development of a distinctive trading that —

• Will be a system based on service, equity and justice drawing its driving force from these values applied in love. It will be distinctive in its overall effect, though not necessarily in every individual application, from a system based on profit maximization or personal gain.

• Will regard the existence of gross material inequities between peoples, where some are without the basic means to enjoy health, security and opportunity for personal fulfilment and development, as a condition to be remedied through the economic system and not perpetuated by it.

• Will regard all commercial decisions, processes and structures as stemming from the ethical and practical framework for love in action to be found in the life of Jesus Christ. It will announce good news to the poor, proclaim release for prisoners, recovery of sight for the blind and freedom for the broken victims. It will feed the hungry, give drink to the thirsty, house the stranger, clothe the naked, support the ill and visit the prisoner.

• Will not exploit customers by depending on their goodwill to excuse poor service or misleading them so that they give support that would not be forthcoming if they had the full facts.

By making the development of fairer trading systems an objective, we recognise the inequity of present systems. Many of these systems are entrenched in national and international laws and conventions as well as being the result of personal selfishness and greed. We recognize that changing some systems will mean changing those laws and conventions where national or political self-interest has been put before the good of all and the rights and interests of the poor.

Traidcraft will regularly consider, in discussion with its staff, directors, shareholders, representatives, producers and supporters, the extent and nature of political lobbying and campaigning that will support its practical trade campaigns and long-term objectives.

Just Trade = Developing People's Potential

Traidcraft recognizes that all people are made in the image of God. We will seek, in our work with producers, with our own staff and supporters and with our customers, to enhance the creative liberating potential of each individual as well as that of the community.

• *Producers.* Many of the workers in craft groups have great expertise that is rarely reflected in the crafts Traidcraft buys. We should aim not

110

only to develop the 'mass production' potential of the groups but also craftsmanship and individual talents.

It is important that producers with whom Traidcraft works are allowed and enabled to achieve their own differing growth rates without pressure resulting from Traidcraft's growth putting at risk their viability, integrity or social concerns and care for their workers.

Traidcraft plc and the Traidcraft Exchange will provide development support services to producers who request practical help in achieving their growth potential, in terms of diversification and product quality as well as production volume.

To ensure that this objective is achieved Traidcraft will be methodical in applying the 'producer criteria' to suppliers and will seek to obtain regular, objective evaluations of the benefits to artisans.

● *Staff*. Greater attention to and investment in staff training is required to allow staff to undertake existing work more effectively and to cope with the increasing demands likely to be put on them through future development. Attention needs to be given to broadening experience through job exchanges internally and with similar organizations. Overseas experience is particularly useful and participation in study tours and overseas work placements or exchanges should be encouraged. Staff understanding of development issues and their role as Christians in the development process must also be expanded.

● *Customers*. Developing their potential will involve improving and increasing our educational work. It should be aimed, in different ways, at reps, mail order customers, shop customers and the general public and should aim to achieve the following:

To make people be so aware of trading issues that they will buy from 'just sources' and be prepared to pay more.

To educate people about the Third World including those who appear uninterested

To help people understand the consequences of materialism and see their lifestyle in a global perspective

To help people understand that the Kingdom of God and its values are relevant and practical

To help educate the electorate towards voting for governments that are concerned for love and justice

To challenge complacency in churches and replace it with a determination to make a stand for issues of love and justice

To provide press releases and material for media coverage of issues

To provide unions with information that will enable them to be more internationally aware and prepared to take informed action across national boundaries

To enable reps and other supporters to influence their own communities

To encourage the adoption of our policies as the standard for all trading companies

We should recognize that to achieve the first two of these objectives in particular will require Traidcraft to operate an efficient service to customers so that they have a positive experience of just trading.

Just Trade = More and Better Jobs

Traidcraft will seek through its development of the market for products from developing countries to create the opportunities for more jobs and better jobs. These criteria apply to all work, both in the rich and poor nations. It is recognized that the wide variety in standards and opportunities will need to be assessed locally with an approach in which realism is tempered by love and justice.

By 'better jobs' we mean jobs that provide —

● Fair wages

● Recognition of each person's worth and of the need for the job each person does

● A good match to each person's skills and capabilities whilst encouraging personal development

● Adequate facilities and equipment to do the job to the standard required

● Adequate safety precautions

● Opportunity and encouragement to participate in decisions, to associate in free trade unions where appropriate, and to share in the responsibilities and benefits of ownership.

● A caring and friendly atmosphere and pleasant work environment, wherever possible

● A proper recognition of work-load and the flexibility to be able to cope with imbalances

● Opportunities to take advantage of the skills gained or pay received or saved to go on to other forms of training or employment or self-employment

Some jobs may be regarded as tedious or unpleasant by all. Where possible these should be shared, rotated or consideration given to mechanization. Where mechanization will lead to replacement of jobs, as well as increased efficiency, it should lead to improved job satisfaction for the remaining workers, and workers should only be replaced by equipment if other work is available for them. Great care will need to be taken to ensure that any equipment or technology introduced is 'appropriate'.

Recognition needs to be given to the unpaid jobs done by our 1000 or more voluntary reps and care taken to ensure that where appropriate their conditions of work comply with the above objectives.

Just Trade = Fairer Relationships within Traidcraft

Traidcraft will seek to establish a sense of common purpose in which relationships are free of personal or departmental interest, acknowledging the Christian precept of love by putting the interests of others before our own.

• There should be an open style of management that will encourage the consultation and the participation of staff in the decision-making processes of the company. Reps and producers will be similarly involved whenever possible.

• All staff should be helped to identify their abilities through an effective and fair job-appraisal system and helped through appropriate training to develop their potential.

• The Traidcraft Exchange should be responsible for the maintenance of the overall policy of the company and should be well informed about its activities.

Just Trade = Efficient and Practical Structures

To support the processes that will achieve these objectives the company will establish and refine operating structures appropriate to the fundamental strategy of the business. They will concentrate resources and efforts and ensure the harmonious development of human, capital and physical resources. A key element in assessing the efficiency and effectiveness of the business will be the achievement of determined profit levels, currently a target of 2 per cent of sales retained after tax.

At least when you have a target you know when you are missing it. Without something specific to aim for you can pretend that you have hit the bull every time. Quite understandably the publication of the Traidcraft objectives made people conscious of the areas in which we were falling short. We had always put a major emphasis on people within the company, but the involvement of staff with management issues was an area that was now being questioned.

One of the difficulties seemed to be that staff found a high level of involvement in the decision-making functions of the company quite costly. There is a story about the farm where the animals were so well treated by the farmer that they decided to say thank you by preparing him a slap-up breakfast. 'I'll provide the milk,' said the cow. 'He can have some of my oats for porridge,' said the horse. The chicken said that she would provide two of her largest eggs. 'But what about bacon?' somebody cried, and they all looked at the pig.

There is a big difference between contributing and participating. If staff wanted to participate in the decisions that really affected the company's future they needed to put in a lot of hard work to understand all the background. Participation had become very costly: the company often had to make time for non-management staff to explore issues, and the staff often had to give up time outside working hours. The growing complexity of the company seemed to slow down staff involvement. For the first time I began to wonder whether the exceptionally low staff turnover (less than 3 per cent per annum until then had left for other jobs) might not be a disadvantage. Did we need new people coming in who would look at us from the perspective of the ordinary commercial operation, see our strong points and criticize our weaknesses? Or was the current disinterest in management issues an indication that we had failed to maintain the standards of staff involvement we had set ourselves as we grew from a small company to a medium-sized one?

8

Fair Shares

At the beginning of 1984 we needed to find an extra £250,000 to support the sales opportunities we could see lining up for the rest of the year. Our overdraft with the bank was already stretched to the limit, and although we had made profits for five years and ploughed £140,000 back into the company we still needed more. The company required a great deal of capital to keep it running, but its capital was mostly tied up in stock. I could not help making a comparison with the greengrocer's shop. Very little money had been needed for stock because most of what was bought in the morning at the wholesale market was sold by the evening. Payments by the customers were all in cash, so money for the following day's purchases was set aside and the rest put straight into the bank. Traidcraft could not have been more different.

Often we would pay an advance to our producing groups to help them buy raw materials or pay wages while the goods were being made. The finished products would take an average of ten weeks to reach us. We therefore were not able to restock a popular line quickly, which meant that we had to order our entire stock for a Christmas season nine to twelve months in advance of actually selling it. As most of our sales were through credit accounts a further seven weeks passed before we got paid for those goods. With a greengrocer's shop money equivalent to three days' sales at the very most was needed to keep the stock flowing and the business turning over; with Traidcraft we needed money equivalent to nearer two hundred days' sales. A rough calculation indicated that we needed to have capital equal to 50 per cent of our turnover in a year to lubricate the process of buying and selling.

We saw only one reason why we could not increase our sales by 35 per cent in the coming year: we did not have the money to buy the products and pay the wages. Two years previously one of our directors had suggested to me that Traidcraft could possibly raise money by becoming a public company. I had been strongly opposed at the time, feeling that public companies epitomized the grasping, profit-oriented, devil-take-the-hindmost features of capitalism. Now the idea was raised again from another of our non-executive directors, Geoffrey Hill, then the financial director of the Bible Society and in contol of a multi-million pound budget himself. Geoffrey said, 'Before you dismiss the idea completely why not have a look at just what the requirements are for being a public company? I think you'll have a surprise.'

He was right. Becoming a public company was quite straight-forward and virtually amounted to the passing of a special resolution. But just being a public company did not mean that the cash would start rolling in. Traidcraft had to issue a prospectus describing the type of business that it was in, how it had performed in the past and what it needed to raise money for in the future. There were a number of statutory requirements that had to be met, but nothing that seemed beyond our capacity to meet. If we had wanted to be quoted on the stock exchange then it would have been a different matter, and many other rules would have had to be taken into account.

Not for the first time we found that the agenda set by the government gave us an advantage as a company that organiza-tions in the charitable or voluntary sector did not have. A few months earlier the Business Expansion Scheme (BES) had been introduced by the chancellor. As part of the campaign to encour-age wider share ownership it allowed purchasers of shares in companies not quoted on the stock exchange to offset the cost of the shares against their highest rate of tax. We were far too small to go for a stock exchange listing so we qualified as a BES company.

The joint stock company and the stock exchange is a combination that is hard to beat. It brings people who want to invest their capital in business in touch with those businesses who want money for development. The investor can choose which type of business to support — guns or garden centres, bookmakers or baby clothes. The fact that speculation is irretrievably part of the system, together with the venality, corruption and devious practice that accompanies the opportunity to make large sums of money, should not stop us from recognizing the intrinsic value of this gem in the capitalist crown. We therefore decided that we should go back to basics. We would launch a prospectus on the naive proposition that we were offering an opportunity to support good business, the 'good' element consisting of the outrageous proposition of benefitting the disadvantaged rather than the opportunity to accumulate through speculation.

It seemed fitting that even under the most market-oriented government we had known and by using legislation designed to encourage public support for private initiative we could present a share issue that appealed to principles that were fundamentally subversive of much that materialism stood for. R.H. Tawney, the economic historian, made this comment, as applicable today as it was sixty years ago.

> The quality in modern societies which is most sharply opposed to the teaching ascribed to the Founder of the Christian Faith lies deeper than the exceptional failures and abnormal follies against which criticism is most commonly directed. It consists in the assumption that the attainment of material riches is the supreme object of human endeavour and the final criterion of human success. It is the negation of any system of thought or morals which can be described as Christian.

When Chris and I had been involved in starting the vegetable-importing business more than ten years previously we had raised the £7,000 we needed by selling our house and going to live

117

over the shop. The house that we had sold was one that we had bought in a semi-derelict state because it had been used as a joiner's workshop. It dated back to the fifteenth century and was said to have been lived in by John Knox. We dug out the earth floor, uncovered the old roof ties and found that much of what we had expected to be rotten timber was quite sound. It was only the accumulated rubbish of centuries that gave the impression of decay. The renovation cost less than we thought because we did not need a new roof: enough of the cross-ties were reliable enough to enable us keep the main structure in place and cut out the bad wood, whilst building a new framework to replace the old.

In Traidcraft we now found that trying to apply radical Christian principles to commercial systems had a parallel. It was not necessary to bring the roof down; indeed some of the timber was sound enough to take the strain whilst we worked out an alternative structure. In the end, I suspected, a lot of the old wood would prove to be unreliable and need replacing, and there was always the danger of rot invading new material from the old, but at least in the short term it provided an easy way to have comfortable and sheltered working conditions.

Encouraged by this structural perspective on one of the commercial pillars of our society we made arrangements to have discussions with a top national and international firm of accountants, a leading legal firm and a stockbroker. The advice we received was that although what we proposed was technically possible we should really be conducting our activities through the charitable channels to which they obviously belonged. However, if we wished to proceed the work could be done on our behalf for about £60,000. As we came out of the meeting, which had also been attended by our own auditors and solicitors from small, local firms, we made a decision: we would make the arrangements ourselves to ensure that we got what we wanted.

Neither our lawyer nor our solicitor had been involved in a public share issue before, but, as they said, all the requirements were quite plain and they saw no reason why we could not write and issue our own prospectus. Looking back at their decision

I realize how fortunate we were to have professional advisers who were not afraid to tackle big issues in a radical way. There then began a process of informing and consulting with staff, reps, our partners overseas and the organizations we worked with in Britain. We planned to issue the prospectus with our autumn catalogue, and a number of deadlines needed to be met on the way. We eventually decided what had to go in the prospectus by making a collection of a dozen or so prospectuses from other companies and drawing up a list of the features that were common to all of them. Having put all the necessary clauses in we added a few of our own. In early September the prospectus went out. Its opening paragraph must have been unique, it read as follows:

> This is an invitation to participate financially in the work of TRAIDCRAFT and is not an investment for personal gain or profit.

We were hoping to raise £300,000, a very small sum as public shares go. Surprisingly the issue attracted comment in all the major national newspapers. In *The Guardian* James Erlichman wrote the following paragraph.

> A Gateshead company called Traidcraft urgently needs a £300,000 cash injection from new shareholders — but it is offering them in return only 'love, justice and equity'. And equity to Traidcraft means putting a higher value on sharing the world's resources fairly than on its own share certificates. Investors must prefer goodness to greed, and should never expect 'personal gain or profit', the prospectus warns.

Similar features appeared in the *Times, Telegraph* and *Financial Times*. Most were neutral in tone but mixed with a little scepticism. The church press was more complimentary and we were pleased to find out that all the denominational papers gave us a good write-up. We waited, uncertain what the reaction would be, as the opening of the application list approached on 17

September. We need not have worried: the forms flooded in with cheques attached. In a third of the time anticipated we had reached our target and had to start sending money back. Brian confessed to me later that it was one of the hardest things he had had to do — return cheques for £200,000 that had been freely offered! We could easily have raised over £500,000. When we added up the bills for all the costs we had incurred we found that we had spent just over £14,000.

One of the issues that we had had to face up to in offering shares to the public was the dilemma over ownership and control. Although Traidcraft had deliberately set its face against profit maximization as an objective it had some features that might make it attractive to a commercial predator, such as another company in the importing business or even a wealthy charity that wanted to buy into a ready-made merchandising operation. We had to grapple with the problem of protecting ourselves from such a take-over and also get clear our own views on the relationships between new shareholders, the trustees, the board of directors, the staff, suppliers and customers.

The possibility of a take-over was one that we approached in the same way as a young person making a will. We knew that we had a responsibility to protect the original ideals of the organization but the possibility of a serious approach by another firm seemed remote. The mechanism we eventually used was based on the one that was used to safeguard the integrity and independence of the international news agency and information organization, Reuter, when it went public. A total of 160 new clauses in our Articles of Association made us a very prickly organization to tangle with. As with Reuter, the legal infallibility of the mechanism has yet to be tested but, much to our surprise, in the following four years we did have three definite approaches from commercial companies interested in acquiring us. I am sure that it was the complexity of our structure that deterred them all at an early stage.

Protecting ourselves from the world outside was one issue. Dealing with internal relationships of ownership and control was entirely different. At first sight it seemed quite straightforward. The company had approximately 3500 shareholders who had provided the money to develop and support the business. There was a group of trustees to watch over the original principles, a board of directors to discuss and determine the trading policy of the company and staff to carry out that policy through buying goods from suppliers in the Third World and selling to customers in Britain. But what were the rights and responsibilities of each of these groups?

All was not as it seemed. As of 1988, as part of the protective mechanism, we had three classes of shares. There were 50,150 voting shares, 1,325,000 non-voting shares and a single Guardians share. The Guardians share only came into effect if there was a hostile take-over and it meant that certain actions could be blocked. A total of 96 per cent of the voting shares were held by our linked charity, the Traidcraft Exchange, and the rest were shared between three staff who had moved over from Tearcraft in the early days. This division enabled the trustees of the Traidcraft Exchange to have absolute control of the company, because they could control the appointment of directors. However, there were nearly 3500 people who had invested more than £1,400,000 who had no voting rights.

There was one problematic area that we never got to grips with in Traidcraft and that has the potential to cast a blight on the whole business of raising money through shares by limited companies. It is the fact that the companies *are* limited. The shareholder is only responsible for the value of the shares and cannot be sued. Is this ownership without responsibility?

A further aspect that we needed to take into consideration as we balanced issues of justice and participation was the role of staff, customers and suppliers. It was argued that Traidcraft was a means for letting the customer relate to the supplier through buying goods. We had tried to recognize this relationship by nominating one of the directors to have special responsibility for producers and by letting the voluntary reps nominate two directors. The role of the staff as facilitators in this process was recognized by having seven out of a potential eighteen directors drawn from company employees. These arrangements were by no means ideal but they did keep alive debate about participation, ownership and control.

People who have worked in areas where 'empowerment' is a key issue will recognize that having a visibly democratic structure is exceptionally important for any people-centred organization. However, the problem with 'buzz' words or issues is that the louder they buzz the more unintelligible they become. I had seen a number of organizations that had crippled themselves through bitter internal debates about democracy and control and I hoped that such controversies would never become an issue in Traidcraft. Paradoxically, something that I hoped would become important for Traidcraft staff never developed: to the present time there is no union representation within the company.

There are probably not many firms where the personnel director and the managing director have tried over a number of years to build up a union presence. Early contacts with one union did not help when it appeared that the local office had no interest in our little branch. I had two main motives for pushing unionization in the company. First, it was clear that a division between staff and management was becoming more pronounced as the jobs became more specialized. However benign the existing staff thought the management were, the time might come when the staff would need a unified voice to argue their point of view. Also there would be times, say in the case of an industrial accident, when management would be legally constrained from taking a supportive and sympathetic approach.

Second, I felt that Traidcraft itself had something to offer the union movement, but that we had to be involved in it in order to exert any influence. Neither of these arguments cut much ice with the staff as a whole. Eventually, after more than eight years, a staff association was formed, but it did not have links with the wider world. Yet although it was difficult to sell some ideas about involvement to the staff, we found ourselves in a major confrontation with a print union.

As our print and graphics team developed to handle an increasing number of catalogues and quantities of support literature, we established what was in effect a design studio. At that time many larger printers would not handle artwork produced by a non-union source and we approached an appropriate union with a view to our design team's joining. All went well until the question of salaries came up. The union insisted that, given the skills and responsibilities of our team, they should be on much higher rates. We explained that as a company we operated low salary differentials within which the actual salary of an individual was determined by a staff committee and not by management. To pay the salaries suggested by the union would have made one member of the graphics team the highest-paid person in the company. A further problem was that the union asked for an effective veto over all new appointments in print or graphics.

We debated the problem through local and regional officers right up to the general secretary. Although our position was recognized and appreciated, no exceptions could be made. We ended up being 'blacked' and had to have our main catalogues printed in Germany for two years until the climate changed. It was a case of institutional inflexibility on both sides as we defended our unusual pay structure, and the union fought to retain a 'rate for the job' which it had established over many years.

This issue was typical of many in which a minority of staff members muttered that the company had let loose a hare, apparently for the main purpose of chasing and catching it. Other issues that came into this category were debates about women in management, pay differentials and job evaluation. 'It's management's job to manage' was a comment that some people made. It was no use pointing out that this management chose to encourage participation and staff involvement in decision-making.

Over the years we held a long-running discussion about this process and about what exactly constituted 'making people aware'. As the management team expanded we were very conscious that the people who had the most to learn were ourselves. There were no handbooks written about our sort of business to which we could refer. But as we came to understand more about putting love and justice into trade we knew that our principles had to be applied within Traidcraft first of all. Sharing with all the staff and learning together was time-consuming and frustrating as well as rewarding, but we knew that people were watching us.

There were our colleagues in the development agencies who were very sceptical about Traidcraft's work to begin with; there were our customers, the reps, the mail-order purchasers and the shopkeepers; and there were all sorts of people who did business with us incidentally, from the driver of the Tuffnells' parcel container to the bank manager. One thing was clear right at the beginning: when the commercial lemon is squeezed it is the non-productive pips that squeak, and it is very hard to demonstrate that education is cost-effective.

In late 1979 we had a letter from someone who had read about our work and wanted to support us but needed to do so through a charitable channel. Education clearly qualifies as a charitable purpose, but at that time not only did we not have our own charity formed but were hoping to keep all Traidcraft's educational work as an integral part of the business. We came to an arrangement with a friendly charitable trust that it would receive the money from our supporter and in turn pay the part-time salary of Jan Simmonds to develop education work.

A support group was formed consisting of local education professionals and it was chaired by Graham Young, a former Christian Aid staff member who at the time was working as northern regional youth officer for the Methodist church. Jan soon found that the scope for explaining, exploring, learning and communicating was unlimited. However big the budget we allocated to this area of the work, there was always need for more money. We soon came up against the question that everyone in education is asked: how do you know that you are being effective? This issue had even more weight in an organization that needed every penny it had to buy stock, pay the rent or the VAT man.

Traidcraft has specialized in the conscious compromise and combining education with business was one of our best demonstrations of the fact. Nevertheless, there were many people who wanted to see us take advantage of the tax relief offered by the government on charitable donations. We agonized over whether to set up a separate, educational charity. What led us to do so was a real uncertainty about our strength of will to retain a strong educational team if the trading side ever went through a rough period.

In 1981 the Traidcraft Educational Foundation (TEF) was established as a charity with its own body of trustees, some of whom also represented the Traidcraft Trust, which owned the shares in the company. The company pledged support to the TEF through a covenant and channelled all charitable donations and gifts directly into its account. The TEF also set about fund raising on its own account and soon was employing two full-time staff.

The work initially focused on providing information about Traidcraft's overseas partners. It gradually shifted to educating people about trading practices and their relationship to justice and development issues. Building up a profile of our producing groups was very important as the information enabled the company and the customer to know whom they were buying from and be able to relate to the maker of that particular product. Campaigning work was also essential. Tariff barriers, restrictions on textiles and sugar imports, the role of coffee quotas, the reluctance of First World companies to offer appropriate dynamic technology to the Third World and its tendency to buy raw materials rather than processed ones, thereby minimizing employment opportunities, figured largely among the complex issues that needed to be drawn to the attention of the ordinary consumer. We believed that if people knew of the injustices in world trade they would be prepared to pay extra to reduce them.

The TEF gradually expanded and became the Traidcraft Exchange in 1986 when it merged with the old Traidcraft Trust. Graham Young was tempted away from youth work to become its director, and in three years the Exchange has established a strong reputation by concentrating on trade-related educational issues at home and direct assistance and technical advice to small-scale community businesses overseas. At the end of 1988 the exchange had a full-time staff of eight; it worked within Traidcraft as a whole but was technically separate.

There is a very real benefit from having an organization within an organization in this way. The trustees of the Traidcraft Exchange have responsibility to see that the trading company, Traidcraft plc, continues to meet the objectives for which it was established. The Exchange lies outside the management structure of the company yet its director is a participating member of Traidcraft's executive management team. Because of these close links the trustees can be sure of being well informed about the internal workings of the company. The Exchange has been able to sponsor many exciting initiatives such as research into an Alternative Bank, the sponsoring of a multi-agency, one-acre theme area at the 1990 Gateshead national Garden Festival, and the appointment of a 'theologian in residence' at the company.

The Exchange has also been able to act as a 'think-tank' on complex issues of principle. It has presented papers on the nature of compromise, on payment according to need, and on a range of subjects that have influenced the pragmatic management processes of the trading company. There has been conflict when the views of the trustees and the board have differed, but debate has helped direct the company back to its first principles.

As we developed a number of different approaches to explain to the public what our work involved we drew heavily on our experience of the lives and work of our producer partners in the Third World. No one can enter the world of the poor and not be moved by it. Our task, we felt, was not only to communicate the experience of poverty, its injustice and degradation, but at the same time to show how our own increasingly affluent lifestyles are a direct cause of the growing gulf between Third World and the First. My own first experience of India in 1972 had had a major impact, not on my thinking but on my motivation. On my return home I developed a new perspective on my own life.

Not long ago I attended a 'resettlement' conference for people who had worked abroad for some time and had returned to Britain. It was clear that many were finding it hard to adjust. For the most part they had been living in conditions of modest adequacy as they served other people in their community.

Now they were overwhelmed by the pace of self-centred Western materialism, and the most common reaction was to reject the whole lifestyle and seek another placement overseas. But increasingly the West provides the model that all wish to copy and I knew that in all the large cities of the developing countries in which they had been working they would find the same attitude. It confirmed my view that we desperately need to look at our society from the outside if we possibly can and highlighted the importance of our programme of overseas visits that had been going on since 1979.

As the Tearcraft reps scheme developed, a number of people asked if there was any way in which they could visit the people who made the goods that they were selling. In 1979 Jan Simmonds planned and led the first study tour to India and Bangladesh, and since then nearly two hundred people have had the chance to meet the people whose goods they sell. The company also subsidized study-tour places for staff who would not normally travel abroad in the course of their jobs so that, by 1988, over a third of Traidcraft's permanent staff had been able to visit several of the main producing partners.

Jan is proud of her record. 'I haven't lost anyone yet' is her claim, although there have been some close calls. A briefing day given three months in advance of departure convinces people that they are not going on a holiday. The average tour covers 15,000 miles using every form of transport, and a typical day starts at 6.30 a.m. and ends at about 10 p.m. The group may see the inside of a hotel for two or three days but mostly stays in basic guest houses, in homes or on charpoys on a mud floor. One returning rep described the experience as 'a low profile antidote to tourism'.

Travel certainly broadens the mind and leaves an indelible impression at the same time. Travellers from Traidcraft have experienced fire, flood and earthquake. They have been through coups, curfews, violent strikes and riots. They have struggled with corruption and stood helpless in the face of death and injury through carelessness. These things do not happen all the time, but many of them are the ordinary lot of people in the Third World.

Return visits have been arranged as well. Traidcraft arranged a number of 'market experience courses' for organizers from a wide range of producer groups. As well as meeting commercial buyers from big stores and seeing goods arrive and go through other processes before they reached the customer the visitors were able to form a general impression of the sort of market into which they were selling. They visited the main trade fairs as well as development organizations such as Oxfam. The participants all stayed with families and in addition took part in a number of seminars on marketing, sales and catalogue design. They all commented on the choice and variety of goods that were available in Britain and the ease with which they could be obtained.

I talked with one visitor from Bangladesh about how the ready availability of mass-produced goods in this country affects the amount of effort that is put into the production of handicrafts. 'If a rich person orders a tapestry hanging for their wall or carved door for their house then they have to seek out the craftsman and tell them what they want. The final product may be a little dirty or slightly the wrong shape. If it is, the local buyer will be angry but will know that the workshop is part of the house and that it is difficult to keep things clean in the monsoon. The person will also understand that insisting on a replacement will make life very hard for the supplier who will have to go through the whole involved process again. But here there are so many shops, all full of things that are nicely wrapped. If you get a bad one then you take it back and the shop gives you another. I have tried to explain this to the women I work with but they just cannot understand.'

Towards the end of 1984 this problem of quality control showed up in a big way. Supplies from the major group that produced wooden products for us were found on arrival to be below standard. We were faced with a dilemma. Up to 30 per cent of the items were too bad to send out to customers, but if we asked for compensation from the producing group for the poor quality goods, let alone the lost sales, it would ruin them. On the other hand if we did nothing then the poor quality might continue. In the end we did decide to withhold a proportion of the payment, but at the same time arranged for our warehouse manager to spend two weeks in Delhi helping the supplier to establish a new warehouse with better quality checking and packing facilities. Unlike many importers of Third World goods we had a commitment to our producers to help them build up their businesses and overcome production problems and would not play the 'survival of the fittest' game by moving on to another supplier as soon a problem arose.

Sometimes our good relationships with the producers became a source of confusion. For years one of the best selling lines has been stone boxes from a group of craftspeople in Agra. Mr Sharma, one of the organizers who works with this group, telephoned me from Delhi about an urgent order for some 25,000 pieces. 'Now, Mr Adams, how would you like the boxes packed: in threes or in sixes?' We had thoroughly discussed this question previously and confirmed in writing between us that threes would be the best. I immediately thought, 'Ah, they must have packed them in sixes by mistake.' As it was more of a preference than a necessity that they be packed in threes I said, 'Well, we would have liked threes but sixes will be perfectly alright.' 'Now, Mr Adams,' came the reply, 'what would you really like?' I was sure by now that they had packed them in sixes so I said, 'Very well, let's have them packed in sixes.' 'Oh dear' said Mr Sharma, 'we have gone and packed them in threes.' The shipment duly arrived packed in threes and we wrote thanking them for their excellent attention to our requirements, but the shipment after that was packed in sixes.

This group in Agra is one that most of the study tours to northern India have visited. They are part of a community that for generations has made earthenware pottery and worked the soft Gorara stone into ornaments and decorative pieces. Traditionally the people lived in thatched houses beside an open sewage drain. The poor artisans had fallen into the hands of merchants and moneylenders who exploited their skills. As an organization named Tara Projects encouraged them to become more independent, gangs of thugs appeared on the scene intimidating the workers with violence and attempting to disrupt the work. Tara and the stoneworkers persevered and although there will be struggles ahead the people have used the money they have earned to build many proper brick houses including a community house, brick in a large part of the drain, supply filtered water and establish better wages. These improvements have been done entirely by the community, not by 'foreign experts', and their success has given them confidence in themselves and their abilities. The role of Tara and Traidcraft has been to make links in India and Britain that allow their traditional skills to be recognized and supported.

These practical stories about communities, with or without the personal experience of a study tour, have enabled the many people who sell products to relate them to real people. It is more difficult to reconcile people with producers who hold political views that are different from their own. For six years Traidcraft has been selling coffee from Nicaragua and for the last four years, sweets from Cuba. Some people are angered at these links and Traidcraft has been accused of being 'political'. Whenever I have received such a complaint I have usually been able to regard it as a compliment. The company is not a charity and has every right to take a political stand. The degree to which we have allied ourselves with a particular political position has been controlled by two things: the extent to which our involvement is able to promote love and justice in trade, and the ease with which the issues could be clearly explained to the public.

From time to time all the main development agencies with which we cooperated asked Traidcraft to tone down material for a catalogue that we were producing for them or amend labels on a product that we were providing for them to sell. The uncertain position of charities concerning political comment and action is likely to remain a difficulty for the foreseeable future. This reticence on the part of the majority makes it all the more important that some strong organizations speak out on political issues when necessary.

9

Justice by Design

'Did you know that Britain is now importing £500 million worth of clothing from the Third World, all of it from sweat shops? What are you going to do about it?' This comment was made to me by one of our more enthusiastic reps at a meeting in the summer of 1985. Until then our attempts at selling clothes had been half-hearted and not very successful. But now I had an answer. 'I'm pleased to say that we have just agreed to embark on a long-term programme to produce a full clothing range; you'll have to wait a couple of years but it's on the way.'

We knew that clothing was in a category of its own. Unlike other products in our range it revolved around fashion trends. The 'ethnic' look had gone out with flower power and showed little sign of returning. This meant that any attempt to enter the clothing market would have to involve designers who knew the trends as well as professional pattern cutters and textile technologists. We would also have to get to grips with the minefield of clothing quota restrictions that severely limited Third World imports.

Such a decision needed the backing of all the members of the board as we foresaw several years' work before the project was likely to break even. We were able to move ahead with some confidence because our new marketing director, Richard Evans, had joined us with extensive experience of small-scale Third World textile groups. In addition we recruited Abi Garner who had just qualified in textile process engineering. Perhaps it would be more correct to say that Abi recruited us. She phoned me up out of the blue determined to sell to us the idea of working with small textile producers in the Third World. She had an easy task as we were already well on the road.

The development of the clothing range was Traidcraft's first major move into basic product development on a large scale. Until then we had modified product design here and there or suggested technical improvements, but most of the craft range had been developed by the producing groups themselves. Some of the products we sold had been designed many years before and their predecessors could even be found in antique shops. But the novelty of ethnic crafts was wearing off and they were being imported on a much larger scale than previously. We realized that all our craft producers would need major design and development input in order to survive. The clothing programme was one in which we provided a great deal of input, and I think it is worth telling in detail. To do so I have drawn to a large extent on Abi's own words, culled from reports she wrote for Traidcraft about the development of the project over the first eighteen months. Her writing gives a flavour of the excitement and the frustrations.

My role has essentially been one of creative communication. I have spent five periods of between two and three months each in India and Bangladesh, with a few days here and there in towns and villages all over the two countries. One little village south of Calcutta was visited five times.

The purpose of my first visit was to be introduced to the textile groups already contacted by Traidcraft, assess their ability to make clothing for the UK market, see how much support could be offered during the process and bring back samples of their work, together with an idea of how they wanted to develop it.

In the first two weeks my eyes were opened to the sights and smells of India and the rich contrasts between one region and another. Straight away I was in the homes and workplaces of the poor, the weakest sector in society.

I was overwhelmed by the warmth, love and courage of the people.

The groups varied tremendously in their size, structure, maturity and need, and that was before considering what they made. There was the small group of women tailors sitting behind sewing machines supplied through Christian Aid funding but totally unable to make use of the low quality cloth being produced by the weaving unit next door. With no concept of what it meant to work they wandered in and out all afternoon. Then there was the joyous team of fifty or so Calcutta women from the most run-down part of the town industriously appliqú-ing the most beautiful skirts. The invaluable forum that their workplace provided enabled them to support one another in the difficult areas of their lives such as dowries and the stories of wives being burnt. Their voice was stronger when they could work together, and several years of being involved in Self Help Handicrafts meant they were standing on their own.

Abi went on to visit a major cooperative in Madras called Co-optex. I had visited them myself the previous year and been impressed with the wide range of smaller textile groups that they were helping. My colleagues, knowing my flair for style, had banned me from ordering any clothing on that visit but tea towels seemed a safe bet, particularly as the stitching was done by a group of handicapped women. Over the previous fifty years Co-optex had helped literally millions of village weavers to shake themselves free of oppressive local merchants who owned their looms and controlled prices. Now they were helping them face the increasing challenge of both modern technology and the protective barriers established by most countries to safeguard their own textile industries. Co-optex was keen to work with us on planning fabrics to our own colours and designs, ideal for what Abi was hoping to do.

I could design my own fabric colourways to be woven by hand in the villages of South India. Now we were in a position to offer tailoring work to a suitable group. Dismissing the commercial factories, Mr Nagarajan of Co-optex mentioned the group of women who had worked on the tea-towel order the previous year. Into a rickshaw and off we trundled to the other side of town. Up the sun-scorched steps we went, into a dark hall: the electricity was off again. Inside there were two rows of women behind their treadle sewing machines, their shy faces showing awe and wonder as a foreigner walked in and transformed an ordinary day.

Disabilities such as deafness or a deformed ankle make a girl from an ordinary Indian family difficult to marry, and she becomes a burden. A local voluntary organization had trained these girls in tailoring skills so that they might have some opportunity to earn their own living. I looked at the work and saw the tatty sewing, the puckered stitching. Then I looked back to the earnest faces and my heart melted. I joined in with them there and then. Through simple language and much gesticulation I came to understand their circumstances. The sewing was bad, they told me, because of the pittance they got paid. They had to work at a frantic pace just to earn enough to eat and there was never enough left over to service the machines.

When I returned on my own a month later there was a welcome chalked on the doorstep. I felt more able to fit into their ways now, and they placed flowers in my hair as a token of friendship. I laid out my pattern on the table; everything was done with smiles and hand gestures. We plodded through the cutting-out step by step: 'They all have to be the same for England, you know.' Then I took the fabric to the nearest empty sewing machine and sat down. They all gathered round as I began to treadle with my feet and guide with my fingers, just as I had done on my own £5 machine at home. As I worked I wondered just what I had to offer: should I really be sitting in that room?

'Neat and quick, sister,' one of them said. The rest were just nodding and pointing. All day we worked in that dark room. I shared their lunch when they sat and scooped out their rice from their boxes, eating of course with their hands. That was just one of the experiences. Each group was so different: the personalities of the leaders, the facilities, the hand batik, the cross-stitch; in each town a different hotel room surrounded me. In the evenings, often too daunted by the prospect of eating alone, I fed off my daily memories and feelings, washed them down with the odd tear of loneliness and went to sleep sprawled under the fan.

One of the problems that we had been aware of when we set up the clothing project was the need for staff to travel. By this time Traidcraft had several seasoned travellers, and we were agreed that three weeks was the optimum length for a business visit. This was normally twenty-one days of work, often starting early and finishing late. It was also our policy to stay in adequate but basic accommodation so the luxuries of five-star hotels were not available. We knew, however, that Abi would need to spend much longer periods of time overseas, often living in the villages. Providing support for staff doing this type of work was certainly a problem for us. However we had been establishing very good relationships with the field staff of the main development agencies and Oxfam and TEAR Fund were particularly helpful in this respect.

When Abi got back to Gateshead after that first visit she had a suitcase full of pieces of fabric. The original list of twenty-five possible groups had been cut down to sixteen, and it seemed as if it might be possible to involve them all in the production programme for the patterns that were coming from the top-class professional designers we were working with in London and Newcastle fashion schools. Abi realized the problem.

It was not an easy jigsaw at all. A 'fully co-ordinated' clothing range for a largely unknown group of customers. I was determined to do something for everyone — young, old, adventurous or otherwise — and it all had to hang together on the pages. A skirt from a Bombay slum, yes, that would go with the Bangladesh village cloth. The pieces began to fit together. Shortly the letters of step-by-step instructions were ready to send, each composed in the knowledge of the capabilities of the group to which it was going. Their needs came first, and communication was the key to getting the work done.

On my second trip the bonds were stronger, the warmth of their faces went deeper into me — and the products were beginning to form. Some samples looked super, but others had arms too short, collars messy, colours varying, cloth too thin . . . The reservations seemed endless. Some of the groups really tried my patience: the workers from one group in Madras insisted that they knew this and they knew that; I really had to shout to make them hear, and it was exhausting.

I spent three days in a village without electricity down near the Bangladesh delta. The women here had not worked before, and I felt an enormous weight of responsibility. I was there on my birthday and as I awoke I felt I had so much to get across. But as the day wore on I again questioned whether I really had anything to offer. However, we managed. The pieces of cloth, the stitches, the noise of the machine became our language, punctuated by grunts and smiles. We even began to learn each other's names.

Abi had spent more time in face-to-face work with people in the villages than anyone else in Traidcraft up to that point. This amount of liaison work was necessary because what we were seeking to do was blend local skills, materials and motifs with contemporary Western designs and colours. Two years previously I had been involved in long arguments with my counterparts in German and Swiss alternative trading groups concerning the corruption of Third World artistic traditions by pandering to Western tastes. They wished to present ethnic crafts to a European public who would be educated into liking them. I understood perfectly well that fashion taste could be adjusted and that in fact it was constantly being manipulated from season to season by the fashion industry. But we did not have the resources to shape public opinion in the same way and we wanted to train poorer people in skills that would bring them a good income.

As Abi brought the skills and materials together we began to plan how we were going to sell the range. We were conscious that we were moving into an area of intense competition. We knew the skill with which fashion catalogues were put together, and we also knew that the big mail-order houses expected 40 per cent returns on conventional merchandise supplied by established manufacturers. But in May 1986, one year after we had launched the project, we took the plunge and began to place orders, knowing that we would have to wait another nine months to see if the range would sell. We started designing a special catalogue to be launched in March 1987. Another set of problems now began to emerge.

Although there was a general feeling that cheap Third World imports were destroying the British clothing industry the facts did not bear this out. Of the 450,000 jobs lost in this area between 1972 and 1983, half disappeared because manufacturers bought new high-tech equipment. The remaining 225,000 jobs were indeed lost to imports, but only a third of those garments came from the Third World. Nevertheless there were severe restrictions on clothing from developing countries that were set out in an agreement called the Multi-Fibre Arrangement. This agreement restricted Third World imports, but left industrial countries free to trade amongst themselves. The share of clothing imports from developing countries had in fact fallen by 20 per cent in the ten years from 1976.

Another problem was that conditions in many Third World clothing factories were appalling. Pay could be as low as 7p an hour, unions were often banned and safety provisions were non-existent. To change all this was a mammoth task. The very structure of the clothing industry worked against it: retailers and wholesalers needed to work with high margins to cover losses caused by swings in fashion. The result was either high prices for the customer or low payments to the producer, often both. But we had to start somewhere and show that change was possible.

We asked Co-optex to assist us as much as possible with

the details of the international trade, as it was experienced in applying for export quotas. Our responsibilities included supplying sizing labels for the clothing, providing washing instructions, setting standards for packing and pressing and ensuring that the whole production process was going smoothly. We had taken a risk and commissioned about half of the cloth from hand-loom weavers in Tamil Nadu, mostly from the village of Melkaluthur. A proportion of this cloth had to be sent on to be cut and tailored in Bangladesh. Abi takes up the story.

I discovered that they hadn't got it done in time, and the fabric was late leaving for Bangladesh. This meant postponing my third trip until the fabric arrived. But worse was to come. In their haste to send the cloth when it was produced the shipment had been dispatched by Co-optex without the necessary documents. There was no way Bangladeshi customs could be cleared without them. Alas, or maybe fortunately, I didn't find this out until I arrived in Bangladesh from India in September. This blow had been preceded by a really encouraging time with the Indian groups. Work was going on everywhere. I was shown piles of clothes neatly packed up and ready to go. 'Neatly' is perhaps a bit of an exaggeration. I could see that some hadn't been ironed, and none of the garments looked as if they had come from the shelves of Marks and Spencers, but there was nothing I could do about it at that stage.

The positive results of our working together were to be found everywhere I went. 'I thought my smile was going to burst,' I wrote in a letter home after a visit to Women's Voluntary Service again. By now I was an old familiar friend. The room was not a sea of faces but a group of familiar people with whom I had worked — together we had moved forward. There were measuring charts all over the walls and the tape measure was used every time. Every single seam of every single shirt was made so conscientiously. The joy amongst the women was amazing. They had earned more in the previous three months than they ever had before and the pride in their work and its quality outstripped anything I could have imagined. The view of Mr Nagarajan, Co-optex's export manager, was completely changed. He did not see them as poor women hemming tea towels any more: they were the best tailors in town and he would make sure that they would get more work.

But in Bangladesh I had to face the problem of the shipment without documents. If I had realized what this meant then I think I would have gone home straight away. But I kept imagining a half-empty catalogue and I knew that we had to get samples for photography. The fabric just couldn't stay stuck in Chittagong docks. However, I kept hearing the same admonition: 'You have made a procedural error, madam.' The next eight weeks were chaos and agony as I struggled with the Bangladeshi bureaucracies. A young white woman who speaks no Bengali says that she has been helping our country: how on earth do we believe that? So into another room of piles of papers, enormous desks with nothing on them except paperweights and huge fans flapping the calendars on the walls. Heads turned: white women do not traipse into government offices uninvited. But I sat down and tried to explain. I explained and explained and explained, to one person after another. 'Yes madam, we will help you. I will ring you on Thursday.' It went on and on. The phones were broken; I hadn't offered any money; sentiments changed. I was back to square one.

The time came when I realized that we weren't going to get fabric in time for photographic samples. Ironically it seemed as if my weeks of pestering were actually going to result in a change to the regulations, but getting the fabric was still going to take time. I could not go back to the UK empty-handed. The only way seemed to be to get more fabric from India, bring it into Bangladesh, get the samples made up and carry them back to Britain.

In Gateshead we had been keeping in touch with this situation and exerting what pressure we could through the Bangladesh

High Commission. It was all complicated by the strained relations between India and Bangladesh. Reliable communication between Dhaka and Calcutta, 120 miles apart, was by air alone. Direct communication by post, telex or telephone between the two countries could be ruled out: it was quicker via London. So we co-ordinated a complex trip in which someone from Madras would travel to Calcutta with a parcel of fabric and meet Abi who would attempt to get out of Bangladesh and back again without a visa.

As I sat on a roof in Calcutta I reflected on the chaotic state of the garment trade. I now understood how a lot of the chaos was in response to the controlling forces in the West: forces that knew little and cared less about what was happening. I just had to sit there and wait for the fabrics, praying that they would turn up on time. Thankfully all went smoothly. I used my charm at Dhaka customs and I was back with my precious bundle. My flight to Britain was two days later so I had to travel straight down to the Kumudini Welfare Trust's clothing factory and shove the material under the machines. At last they were making one garment . . . but they had no buttons! The day before I left found me sitting in the marketplace sifting through the buttons at the button stall.'

Abi returned to a hero's welcome at Traidcraft, and we rushed the samples into the photographic studio. All our catalogues were designed from start to finish on the premises and our own staff acted as models. This approach was a distinct advantage when time was short. In the event the catalogue was two weeks late and some of the clothes shipments even later, but we had launched a new range. Variations in patterns, colours and sizes gave us a total of seventy-nine different garments, from a T-shirt to a silk dress. They were all made by community groups from fabric woven by hand. In the catalogue there were features on the producers, photographs of them at work and details of their lives and expectations. There was a picture of a lady from Women's Voluntary Service stitching up a cotton beach set alongside one of Sean Murphy, our warehouse supervisor, wearing the garment and proudly displaying his hairy legs.

By the time the clothes from the first catalogue were on sale the second year's range was already being designed. The main fashion designers determine clothing trends at least a year in advance so working with Third World groups to this time scale is possible if you obtain good design advice. There were many problems still to overcome in presentation, quality, sizing, and uniformity of material, but we had made a good start. Traidcraft has now produced three main clothing catalogues and sold more than £600,000 worth of garments. Third World fashion shows have become a part of the voluntary reps' way of selling and communicating, often reaching a completely new type of customer.

Clothing was not the the first product range to have a catalogue to itself. At the beginning of 1986 we had launched a catalogue offering over sixty types of recycled paper products. We had first offered recycled paper for sale in our main Christmas catalogue in 1983, and demand for it had grown steadily. Not only did it provide an opportunity to point out the need for a responsible use of the earth's resources, but the Traidcraft name and address printed on the envelopes, re-use labels and Christmas cards became our biggest single source of new customers. Wrapping paper with designs based on traditional Third World motifs became one of the bestselling lines. We also made an offer that for every two exercise books purchased from us we would donate one to an educational project linked with our producing groups.

We had established a paper-conversion unit to produce most of our recycled paper products. This unit is not a machine that pulps waste paper and regurgitates it as new; that is still mostly done in large mills, and an increasing number are installing facilities for recycling. Our unit comprised a guillotine, paper-counter, pad-making carousel and drill; it gave us the capacity, when combined with our print room, to turn out a wide variety of stationery.

Although sales of Third World products increased each year,

they represented a decreasing proportion of our total sales as paper, books and other promotional products were introduced. There was a continuing debate about whether we should sell ball-point pens made in Birmingham just because they had 'Traidcraft' written on the side. Were we meeting our objectives by including a made-in-the-UK pottery mug with our slogan on? There was a feeling that these products were somehow diverting attention away from our main purpose of supporting Third World economies.

From the vantage point that comes with the passing of time I think it is possible to see that there was a real public trend towards the purchase of products that were going to build a sustainable rather than an exploitive economy. For one thing, customers sympathetic to the needs of the Third World were also likely to be aware of other global issues. But there was another factor: many customers probably supported Traidcraft because it was 'a good thing' and they would agree to buy goods for which they might only have a marginal use. In spite of their goodwill, it was becoming increasingly clear that much of the craft range was 'tired' and needed a major overhaul if it was to stay in the mainstream. More and more technical, design and marketing support would have to be provided for Third World producers and Traidcraft itself would have to take more seriously the transfer of appropriate resources.

10

Loss of Confidence

At the beginning of April 1985 the prospects for Traidcraft seemed very rosy. We had just had an amazingly successful share issue, and our worries about funding the rapid growth of the company were over. We had a large warehouse with plenty of space for expansion, we had just made a net profit of £37,000 and made covenanted payments of £38,000 to support educational and development work outside the company. Sales had exceeded £2 million in the previous year, and we had reached an agreement with CAFOD, the Catholic Fund for Overseas Development, to produce a catalogue in its name for widespread distribution. It was with considerable confidence that we budgeted for sales of £2.9 million. In fact, during the next two years we were to suffer losses of £370,000 and face a difficult period of self-doubt and uncertainty.

That summer we worked on our first strategic plan for the company. As we stated in the introduction we were looking 'at the processes which will make things happen'. We tried to introduce the idea of two types of funding within the business: operational funding, the money needed to keep the current business going at a successful level; and strategic funding, money which would develop new projects and look for long-term results. The Traidcraft range of products had been steadily growing and becoming more diverse. There were now more than 350 craft items that we were importing from 60 producers and 97 food items from 24 suppliers. We were also selling 144 different types of paper products, cards or books. We set out a programme of support for existing suppliers and the development of new ranges, in particular the clothing range. We had planned sales of £2,900,000 for the financial year and had built up our staff and development programmes based on that figure. In the event we were some £200,000 short of our forecast and returned a loss £61,000 after paying out a modest dividend.

The orders had flooded in as usual during the autumn of 1985, and to begin with we appeared to be on target. However, a corresponding quantity of parcels was not leaving the dispatch bay. A number of factors combined to create what became a serious problem. Monsoon rains in India had ruined one major shipment as it awaited loading at the docks; our major supplier of dhurries had suffered a disastrous fire; the quality of some rattan goods from the Philippines was extremely poor and could not be dispatched; and we had severely underestimated the demand for several of our bestselling items. As a result we received more than £250,000 worth of orders that we could not fill.

Although we had lost nearly 10 per cent of our sales in this way we were still experiencing rapid growth. During that autumn we handled 30 per cent more orders than in the previous year and weaknesses began to appear in our processing system. A number of computer failures in both our hardware and software meant a return for a while to manual processing of orders. We were picking and packing our orders by using supermarket baskets and trolleys, and a number of inefficiencies began to show up in this area as well. It seemed that we had been able to provide for the company financially by the share issue and thereby raise funds to expand into a large warehouse with room to grow, but our operating systems had not kept up.

I knew that as a manager I had not kept on top of the demands generated by a rapidly-growing company. I invited two experienced management consultants sympathetic to the aims of the company to review our structure and our team. I think that we were all surprised at the positive report that they gave. We were told that we had a competent and well-balanced staff, but it was clear that we had to look very hard at what the business would need in the coming year.

As we reviewed the previous twelve months we still saw record sales, but we also saw record levels of customer complaints, a record number of orders that we could not fill, and a very slow turn-around time for the orders that we had supplied. Our 1986 strategic plan included specific plans to remedy these weak points.

We decided to mechanize our picking and packing system with conveyors and new racking whilst substantially altering our computer software by writing our own systems using three skilled computer staff. We ordered products from our partner groups further in advance and in larger quantities to avoid going out of stock. We established a better system for handling queries and allocated more staff to customer service. At the same time we continued our work on developing new product ranges. Autumn 1986 arrived with the company much better prepared for a busy Christmas, but it soon became apparent that we were just not getting the orders we had expected.

We had planned for sales of £3,675,000, an increase over the previous year of 36 per cent, reckoning that our growth rate of 30 per cent would continue and that we would be able to supply a good part of the orders we had lost the year before. We had not reckoned with the effect of our poor performance in 1985 on our customers. Disillusioned by late arrivals and incomplete orders many customers just did not come back to us for their Christmas gifts. Our sales were £500,000 down on expectations by Christmas, and our board of directors had serious questions to ask of management.

'At the time of writing the position of finance director is vacant and there is an urgent need to make a suitable appointment to this position.' Those who turned to the strategic plan produced in the early autumn of 1986 may have picked out this sentence as a highly significant one. Earlier that year we had realized that the load that Brian Hutchins was carrying as director responsible for both finance and all the operational (warehouse, packing and dispatch) aspects of the company, was excessive. We had therefore created two posts, finance director and operations director, with Brian taking over the second. We believed that we had made a good appointment to the finance post, but a few days before taking up the job the person concerned had second thoughts and withdrew. We therefore went through our most difficult sales period with Brian and I trying to handle our finances.

Fortunately we had found a new head of finance by Christmas. Philip Angier had been a banker in the City of London before 'dropping out' to become resources officer for the Anglican diocese of Liverpool. Philip had bought shares in the first issue and had been elected a non-executive director that summer by the non-voting shareholders. He later told me that at his first board meeting the opening item was the statement that we needed to start looking for another finance director. 'I spent the rest of the meeting wondering whether to apply,' he said. He did, probably not realizing that he was to take on the most difficult job in the company for the next eighteen months.

Ray Skinner, who had been our chairman since the beginning, had concerns of his own as well as those of Traidcraft. He had been the vicar of nearby Newbottle for ten years and felt that it was time to move on. Ray had been interested in increasing dialogue between Christians and Muslims ever since the time he had spent in northern Nigeria twenty years previously. As chairman and managing director respectively, we used to hold regular meetings at the Black Bull midway between our homes. One evening, after running through the papers for the coming board meeting, Ray said, 'Well, I've taken the plunge: I think we'll be leaving next Easter.' I suggested that the scope for missionary work in Saudi Arabia was rather limited. 'I know,' he replied. 'That's why we're going to Oman.' And sure enough he did, as chaplain to the Protestant church. He was difficult to replace, for Traidcraft was now a complex company demanding a high level of business and personal skills in its senior officers.

At the same meeting Ray and I also talked about a phone call I had had earlier in the week from Greenpeace. They told me that they were expanding at a phenomenal rate and had not had a particularly good experience with their mail-order catalogue that Christmas. Would we be interested in taking on the job of building it up for them? Although on the one hand this invitation immediately struck me as a great opportunity I could see all sorts of problems. We had just been through a very bad sales period ourselves and would have to make cut-backs in the coming year. Would the board see the Greenpeace project as just a diversion of management time away from Traidcraft's real business? Also there would be many amongst the staff who would see a link with Greenpeace as either watering down our commitment to the Third World or getting too involved with an organization that did not share the same beliefs.

As it turned out the programme that we developed with Greenpeace looked good from all angles. We offered them a much better class of service than they had had before and they added a lot of Traidcraft products to their range of promotional merchandise. Our completely re-written computer system had played a big part in clinching the contract, and we were told that it compared very favourably with the ones used by some of the really big mail-order companies ten times our size.

It was very important to me that Traidcraft was beginning to spread its wings and look at broader environmental and consumer issues. We were still seeing strong growth in our food range and recycled paper, but sales of crafts were declining. In general the emphasis in the media on 'world problems' was moving towards a consensus on four main issues: over-population, famine, global heating and deforestation. To my mind there was one important omission: over-consumption. It was noticeable that analyses shied away from tackling this issue, for dealing with it risked creating problems for economies that were dependent upon growth and expansion to maintain their equilibrium. Traidcraft needed to make its voice heard on this unpopular topic and I saw the link with Greenpeace as stimulating our policy-making in this area.

It was the one piece of good news in what was turning out to be a very gloomy winter. Christmas 1986 saw the staff pantomime feature some doom-laden scenes, partly as a result of a memo that I had circulated outlining our present position and steps we

147

needed to take to remedy the problems. (If the details of how we set about coping with our situation is something you feel you can skip then you can pass over the next few pages!)

KEY AREAS FOR ACTION, DECEMBER 1986

Although the executive directors review the performance of the company on a continuing basis, special attention has been paid over the last two months to major areas of concern that have emerged as the marketing and operational pattern developed during the peak sales period. This paper is a summary of a series of discussions and reports and is the considered joint view of the executive directors of the company.

● *Our fifth objective*. Traidcraft has a range of objectives, the fifth and final one of which equates just trade with efficient and practical structures. This positioning is deliberate. We believe that the company is ultimately of passing value only unless considerations about fairer systems, the development of people's potential, the creation of more and better jobs and attention to fair internal relationships are an integral part of our work. However, unless our fifth main objective, efficient and practical structures, is realized we will not have the opportunity to demonstrate the previous four. This paper deals primarily with the evidence that our fifth objective is not being achieved at present and suggests some courses of action to remedy problems that have arisen.

● *Weak points*. We can now forecast, unfortunately with some accuracy, that sales will be some £400,000 below our budget for the year. The figures presented in the year-end forecast are based on an estimated final sales figure of £3,272,000. Although variation either way is possible on this figure it is felt to be reasonably accurate. It is probable that a somewhat greater variation will take place on the cost of sales figure forecast and a 1 per cent variation on this figure will result in an adjustment of approximately £40,000.

It so happens that our successful share issue will enable us to absorb a major loss if it does occur, but we need to be clear that this is a 'last chance'. At this stage we can identify the following as probable causes for the reduced sales.

Loss of customers as the legacy of our poor performance last year

Loss of re-orders due to continuing poor performance this year

Rapidly developing lost sales which could constitute 50 per cent of our deficit

Poor product performance

Failure to generate significant new business in mail order and reps

An over-optimistic target figure for the 1987/87 budgeted sales set earlier in the year, partly due to pressure to improve revenue to meet expenditure commitments

All the problems listed above could have been significantly ameliorated by better management. That is not to say that the last year has not seen very major changes and improvements. One has only to see the physical changes in the warehousing and picking and packing layouts, the increasing use of various types of computers, the greater capacity for analysis we now have, the growth in our personnel systems and the emergence of working groups concentrating on particular functions. However, we have to recognize that although significant progress has been made in many aspects of company work, the senior managers of the company and in particular the executive directors have not channelled effort into the critical areas as far as our fifth objective is concerned.

It is particularly worrying to note that, at a time when sales growth has been moderate (only just over half of that forecast) we have not been able to consolidate and improve certain systems. During the last few weeks prepacking, quality control, paper production, packing, catalogue requests, credit control, order forecasting/placing, co-ordination of product development progress and clear direction of our marketing efforts have all been raised as areas of concern.

● *Management audit.* The management structure agreed at the beginning of the year has shown some strengths and weaknesses. In the new structure good working relationships are developing and experience is being exchanged and transmitted in new ways. We are now in the process of auditing our management experience and skills by grouping and department. An early review, pruning unnecessary activity to strengthen other parts and directing resources of the company so that it develops in accordance with our medium term strategy, is now being given more attention by the executive directors.

● *Action.* We have tried to identify a course of action which will deal with the major weaknesses within the company as we see them at the present time. The main points are set out below:

Product supply. We will be rationalizing our product range and in many cases deleting variations on a theme or product style. There will be a reduction of 25 per cent in numbers of individual products sourced directly from Third World producers in next year's catalogue range. We have set targets of 180 products retained from the present range, with higher stocks and higher margins. We will need about 90 new products to freshen up the catalogue presentation and interest existing customers. Ordering will be brought forward and particular attention paid to quality and packing.

We have already begun an intensive assessment of existing product ranges and orders for 150 'bestselling' products have already been placed with the suppliers for next year's catalogue. We have set a target of ordering new products for the main catalogue by the end of January. The overall objective on product supply will only be to offer through the main catalogue products which can be fully supported in terms of reliability of the producer and stock availability. This will mean excluding some existing groups from the main catalogue but their requirements will be met through alternative marketing channels, in particular the extension of the catalogue at present made available to voluntary reps, and a more systematic programme of test-marketing products through our retail shops.

Contribution. Our percentage contribution across our whole product range has effectively been diminishing over the past few years for a number of reasons including reduction in mail order, increase in trade sales and 'buying' sales by paying commission to Christian Aid and CAFOD. This steadily declining gross profit on a rapidly increasing sales target has, as the last two years have shown, made us particularly vulnerable to the effects of failing to meet our sales targets. We have begun a process for the 1987/88 budget of determining our emphasis on marketing through different channels and the composition of our product range by primary reference to contribution rather than sales volume. The estimated contribution for the present year across all channels averages out at 47.02 per cent. This is the key figure which we are working to improve, and our pricing and marketing policies will be designed to raise that by some 2 per cent overall.

We will also change our marketing programme so that the more profitable sales channels get a higher percentage of overall sales. In particular a reduction has been made in the agents category, which is particularly low margin. The effect of this adjustment on sales channels only, without looking at pricing policy on the product ranges, thus improves our contribution by 1.68 per cent.

Considerable work is in progress on working out appropriate price modifications in practice on individual product lines. Our best estimate for the year ending 31 March 1987 shows that although we have some particularly high contributors, we have some exceptionally poor contributors towards overall gross profit, notably ground coffee and the loose teas.

Improvements can be made in the contribution of the product ranges through the pricing mechanism. In addition to improvements in existing strong ranges, a major effort will be made to improve the contribution of the weak product ranges. This is likely to result in lower sales of these product ranges but at a higher margin, and both consequences have been allowed for.

Marketing. Considerable work has been done on a modified marketing policy for 1987/88. The marketing policy naturally needs to tie in with the direction of the emphasis on contribution and this means placing resources at the disposal of the higher-margin sales channels. We are still in the process of determining how resources will be allocated, but it is already clear that the size of the main catalogue will need to be reduced by eight or twelve pages and that resources will have to be made available for methods of selling excess stock not included in the main catalogue. Strategies may include the expansion of the extended catalogue, a special 'bargain' mail-order catalogue, a clearance shop, special trade promotions, etc. It is intended to make the main catalogue available earlier to voluntary reps, by the end of the third week in July.

Product development. We are increasingly recognizing that the company must invest more in product development if it is to bring forward new product ranges and revitalize the main catalogue annually. The budget will contain recommendations to provide additional resources in this area and the appointment of a senior manager to co-ordinate and develop this work will be of particular help.

Budget for 1987/88. As will have been noticed, we are targeting a sales figure of £3,800,000 for 1987/88. Unlike previous years we do not wish to relate our areas of expenditure on the budget to our sales volume figure; rather we wish to direct comparisons towards the contribution from this sales figure. The figure which we are targeting is considerably lower than that indicated in the strategic plan. This target of 16 per cent cash sales increase is lower than our present forecast for the current year of 21 per cent and considerably lower than the forecast in the strategic plan of 30 per cent for next year. Bearing in mind that there will be inflationary price increases included in that figure, the real growth level is not more than 10 per cent. We therefore can categorically say that we are aiming at a very modest increase and offering genuine scope for consolidation of systems.

Conclusion

This paper has attempted to draw together some of the policies which we think should determine the course of the company over the medium term. In some respects it is a change of emphasis and, as will be clear from the above paper, much thinking remains to be done: the headings above outline only an interim position on some of these issues. However, we do believe that we have some clear financial and managerial objectives established and can see our way towards implementing them during the coming months.

That rather turgid memo provides a glimpse of some of the

complexities and issues that we were facing. We had moved a very long way from the structures we had in our first year when eight of us tried to sort out our problems over our morning cup of coffee. Already rumours were going around that the position was so bad that redundancies would have to be made very soon. As we planned the budget we set ourselves the target of holding the salary bill at the same level in cash terms. There were certain savings that we planned to make on overtime and temporary staff, but in fact we did end up needing to lose several jobs. We had a number of discussions with all the staff and it was agreed that we would all have just a £100 pay rise each and increase the hours worked by 5 per cent without extra pay. Given that we did not pay our normal bonuses, staff effectively took a pay cut of more than 10 per cent. However, this strategy enabled us to limit the number of compulsory redundancies amongst the Gateshead staff to one, although we did reduce our staff further by not replacing people who left throughout the year for the range of personal or family reasons that are bound to occur in a group of more than a hundred.

When the accounts were finally published we showed a loss of over £300,000, wiping out all the surplus we had accumulated over the previous seven years. It was true that we had written down our stock extensively and that the buildings which we owned would probably merit a higher valuation, but there was no doubt that the result was bleak. I had been thinking for some months about whether I should resign. After all, the primary responsibility for this sort of loss was mine and, in many people's minds, a big question mark hung over Traidcraft's future. However, by the time of our AGM in July, I was certain that we had got the company back on course. The response of the staff had been magnificent, the work on the Greenpeace contract was going well, the producer and product development team was coming up with some excellent new items and our bank manager was still on friendly terms. At the AGM itself 250 shareholders and voluntary reps turned up to encourage us to keep going and not be too discouraged by the deficit.

Our target in the coming months was to turn a massive loss into a profit, and some very radical proposals had come up at board meetings as to how this might be done. These often involved slashing staff numbers and overheads so drastically that I was convinced that Traidcraft would be left a shell of its former self and with morale so low that the whole character of the company would be changed. As executives we found it hard to convince some of our colleagues on the board that we believed we had analyzed the company's weak points months previously, taken action and were already beginning to see positive results.

Over the August Bank Holiday in 1987 I had been asked to give two seminars on 'Ethics and Enterprise' at Greenbelt, an annual Christian arts festival held near Northampton. Traidcraft had a huge marquee as usual and sold nearly £10,000 of goods, quite a contrast with the £400 worth that Chris and I had sold on behalf of Tearcraft in 1975. Our children Zoë and Lewis had been toddlers then, and they had paddled in the quagmire of the Greenbelt campsite. Now they were serving the thousands of people who came to the Traidcraft tent and I was amazed that hundreds of people came to my seminars. On the way home we called in to see Tim McClure in Birmingham. Tim was now general secretary of the Student Christian Movement; he had also been on the Traidcraft board for three years and had become its deputy chairman.

We talked about trends over the last few years and the fact that since the early 80s students had seemed to show less concern for issues of social and international justice, having been sucked up into the competitive world of getting good grades and securing a job. We sounded like what we were — a couple of '68 radicals bemoaning the lack of desire for change in young people. By contrast there had been a great interest in those offering an alternative view of the economy at the Greenbelt seminars, but how could that enthusiasm be mobilized? 'I think I'm getting stale, Tim,' I confided. 'I need to do something different, come at the issues from a new angle.' 'I know the feeling,' Tim said, 'but don't leave Traidcraft at the moment. You may think that the business is back on course, but precious few others do. They'll think you're leaving a sinking ship.'

We returned home at the beginning of September to find the Christmas season in full swing at Traidcraft as usual. Sales were pretty close to target, costs were being kept down and orders were being turned round in record time with the result that there were very few queries. I sat down and wrote out a dozen good reasons for leaving Traidcraft, put the sheet in my filing cabinet at home and gave myself six months to think it over. I had no idea whatsoever about what I should be doing in the future, just a sense that I should be moving on. At Greenbelt I had been talking about how Christians in particular needed to be open to change and yet I was finding it remarkably difficult to apply this advice personally.

11

Faith at Work

'I don't think that we should invite a heretic onto our premises, let alone ask him to talk to us.' Coping with the different perceptions of the views of David Jenkins, the Bishop of Durham, within whose diocese our Team Valley warehouse lay, was just one of the tensions that we learnt to live with as a working group. Nevertheless I was rather disappointed that when he did spend an afternoon with us his most vociferous critic was on a study tour in India and several others chose to take a half-day's holiday. Our tolerance of differing points of view was less than ideal!

About 85 per cent of Traidcraft's staff were Christians, and they represented every major denomination and tradition. Many people had applied for jobs with us because, as they said, we were a 'Christian company'. Those that were appointed soon found out that we were still trying to discover what that meant. In fact after the first couple of years we stopped using that phrase in our literature and instead said that Traidcraft was a company run by people who wanted 'to apply principles of love, justice and practical action derived from an understanding of the Christian faith'. We reluctantly switched to this rather dry and cumbersome statement because we were finding that there was no area of our work where there was not endless scope for applying our faith yet few areas where we could lay claim to a definitive approach.

The issue that might have been thought to cause the most problems never did. The countries from which the bulk of Traidcraft products came all had minority Christian representation in their populations as a whole. Although we dealt with many producer groups that had been established by missionaries or local churches, most were operated and managed by people who drew their spiritual understanding from Islam, Hinduism or Buddhism. Over the years many people from Traidcraft travelled abroad, and yet faith-to-faith relationships rarely caused difficulties; they were more often a source of strength.

Alongside our Christian affirmation we stated that the company's work was directed towards 'people of all faiths or none'. We emphasized especially service to the poor, underprivileged, disadvantaged and oppressed throughout the world. In this our beliefs as Christians coincided with those of many people of goodwill from other faiths and with those of numbers of people who held a purely secular world view. At the same time we discovered from experience that although the understanding of God in the faiths of the world was very real, there was a mutual confusion: anyone who tried to weld together a 'world faith' with a set of common denominators would be doomed to failure.

There was much in common: all the main faiths were deeply concerned about the problems of suffering and justice; all sought salvation; all recognized that humanity was unable to achieve this unaided; all subscribed to the principle of 'do as you would be done by'. As a group of people involved with translating faith into action, we had that much to share, but then opinions diverged. My own view was that the Christian faith was focused on that ultimate reality, the one God whom we all sought. It seemed to me that the major religions all recognized the nature of God as love and goodness and as the source of redemption, and that in spite of the deceit, evil, superstition and ignorance that surrounded us all our knowledge of God could lead to salvation.

Just as having a glimpse of how it might be possible to bring justice and peace into a divided world was important to me, so it was essential to have a working understanding of humanity's relationship with God. This understanding in turn enabled me to make very positive statements about my own faith. If I saw truth in the faiths of the world, how much more firmly could I say as a Christian that, for me, Jesus Christ and the God of the Bible were the truth.

We all tend to be less tolerant towards our own family than we would be with mere acquaintances, and in the same way our internal discussions about how to reflect our Christianity were often very heated compared with our inter-faith dialogue. The experience with TEAR Fund had shown how concern to be right in our understanding could lead to entrenched positions with little room for compromise. We faced the problem of all new organizations: how to enshrine original principles, make sure that they lasted beyond the first generation, encourage flexibility and yet avoid creating a structure that was either too bureaucratic and legalistic or too dependent upon strong personalities. What eventually emerged was a relatively orthodox, perhaps even conservative framework, with a radical and liberal interpretation.

A religious statement set out our basis of faith in the original deed of trust for Traidcraft. It was, in theological terms, a little to the right of centre. All trustees had to 'affirm' this document; directors and senior staff had to be 'in sympathy'. (One director told me that he felt a great deal of sympathy for it.) But whatever was included constitutionally it was the staff who reflected the underlying ethos of the business. Traidcraft's policy on the appointment of staff was to consider whether they could represent the Christian perspective as needed in their work. Although it sounds like a mechanism for effectively debarring non-Christians from key jobs we found ourselves offering an important post in producer group liaison to a committed agnostic.

I had seen enough 'Christian' organizations to know that the title by no means guaranteed a relaxed, supportive working environment. All people, whether or not they were saints, responded in predictable ways to certain types of management style, and aggressive, hierarchical direction could alienate the most charitable feelings. In many respects secular management theory was far ahead of the best Christian intentions. A widely-accepted analysis of what motivated people in their work had been published in 1960 in the USA by Douglas McGregor. He argued that too many organizations assumed that work was something that was basically unpleasant, in which people have to be strictly supervised and want to be told what to do so that they can avoid responsibility. But it is perfectly reasonable to assume the contrary — that people do not dislike work and that they can be much more powerfully motivated if they are allowed to set objectives for themselves as individuals as well as for the business in which they work and then strive to meet them.

I had been surprised as I worked through my MBA programme to discover just how far contemporary American management theory had already defined personal and organizational approaches in a way that we at Traidcraft had been reaching towards in a very unsystematic fashion. The concern of a business for the personal development of its individual employees was a case in point. The widely-accepted current management approach had not been derived from the pages of the New Testament; it owed more to a hierarchy of needs set out by a social scientist named Maslow and which argued that a person's behaviour, at work or elsewhere, was an attempt to meet these needs. People would usually attend to the lower order needs first: air, warmth, shelter, food and safety were all basics requirements. Then they would try to meet higher-order social needs, such as being loved and accepted. Next, the argument ran, individuals sought recognition and esteem, and finally they sought to fulfil their own potential. The majority of people in our industrial societies now have their basic needs met, but McGregor argued that our business organizations had not generally progressed to meet the higher needs of their employees. The result of this was expressed pithily by top executive Robert Townsend in his bestseller *Up the Organization*.

And look at the rewards we're offering our people today: higher wages, medical benefits, vacations, pensions, profit

sharing, baseball and bowling teams. *Not one can be enjoyed
on the job*. You've got to leave work, get sick, or retire first.

That was written in 1970, and since then many organizations
have made changes to remedy the situation. Today the word
'spiritual' is moving into the language of management. It is used
not in a religious sense but as a catch-all term describing the
dimension of personal fulfilment, purpose and ethical satisfaction that employees should be deriving from their work. This is
not to say that individual Christians and the Christian tradition
as a whole have not played a part in shaping the concept, but
their role has been small, and a global view of work based on
Christian principles is still lacking. The fundamental questioning about the purpose of business activity is only just beginning.
The development of the individual in the workplace has to be
related to the individual without work; the growing concern in
the West for personal fulfilment of the higher needs has yet to
be reconciled with the failure to meet the basic needs of the
Third World.

When Traidcraft moved out of predominantly Christian
circles into the world at large, I was very conscious of how
'Christian language' might alienate people. So Traidcraft, along
with other progressive Christian organizations, sought to avoid
other-worldly phraseology. It is a little ironic that the secular
world chose the same moment to discover that it had neglected
the 'spiritual'. At some point in the last few years we passed one
another, each heading for the place where the other had come
from.

I have mentioned before that Traidcraft found itself moving
into areas where Christian thought had little organized presence. What was noticeable was that others were there ahead of
us. 'New Age' ideas, containing much of value, drew strongly
on Zen, Yoga and Eastern spiritual traditions rather than a
Christian base. Also mixed in were the more problematic areas
of astrology and nature worship. But there were other, more
surprising companions. One of them wrote as follows:

Today our main job is to lift the individual spiritually, respecting his inner world and giving him moral strength. We are seeking to make the whole intellectual potential of society and all the potentialities of culture work to mold a socially active person, spiritually rich, just and conscientious. An individual must know and feel that his contribution is needed, that his dignity is not being infringed upon, that he is being treated with trust and respect. When an individual sees all this, he is capable of accomplishing much.

I read this passage to our Thursday meeting of the full staff early in 1988 and could see that it was getting a good response as being very much in line with the Traidcraft ethos. As I revealed the cover of the book I had been reading from there was some consternation, for beneath the title *Perestroika* was the smiling face of Mikhail Gorbachev.

The presence of numerous and diverse contributors to the debate is at times confusing, but it must be seen as stimulating. Within Traidcraft we had begun the journey of developing theories of just trade, creative working practices and a sustainable economy by looking for guideposts in a 3,000-year-old biblical tradition. As our isolation and naivety diminished we realized that we had many fellow-travellers on the road. We had a lot to learn from them even though we were not clear whether we were going to the same destination. From an initial reaction of seeing other traditions as a threat we began to have more confidence that our own roots — which we saw as prophetic yet relevant for today, idealistic yet practical and spiritual yet grounded firmly in reality — could constructively absorb much of value whilst remaining distinctively Christian.

For many this was not an easy process. The majority of Christians at Traidcraft came from a church tradition that was evangelical and theologically conservative. Much of the company's work, particularly through the reps, was offering a service, a product and a message to a public with a similar background. It was in this context that we spent many hours discussing our Christian identity as a team of people. In some respects we had a microcosm of the church on the premises. If we could not develop amongst us a distinctive working style and approach to development issues that exhibited a global caring then how could we expect to convey such a message to our customers?

Although we could agree on the aim, the methods were another matter. At any job interview we always made it clear to people that the discussion of spiritual issues was on the agenda of the company as an integral part of its work. Worship, where personal commitment was obviously necessary, was optional. Debate, however, was for everyone.

By 1986 the more formal aspects had settled into a pattern. The week began with between twenty and twenty-five minutes of worship. Attendance was voluntary but the meeting was in work time. The eight or so main departments of the company took it in turns to lead the worship. These times were attended on average by about a third of the staff and ranged from the conventional mix of hymn, reading and prayer to drama, meditations and Third World liturgies. A small prayer group met together at Tuesday lunchtime, and at our Thursday morning general staff meeting we would provide an occasional focus on a specifically Christian initiative amongst our programme of general development education topics. This meeting always ended with a short reading, usually with a love, peace and justice theme.

Earlier in the company's life our general meeting had contained both worship and prayer, but gradually the feeling developed, not least amongst the Christians, that we should not force non-Christians to participate. The status of our worship time was a matter of heated debate, with many wanting Traidcraft to affirm its Christian identity in this way. In many respects we had the reverse problem of most Christian organizations. Our practical Christian action and witness was built into our corporate structure, activities and objectives. The more 'symbolic' areas of worship, prayer and 'spiritual' development were those that caused the heart-searching.

The following brief meditation is an example of how we tried to develop material that stemmed from our work experience and yet tried to relate it to both the gospel and the situation of those in the Third World. Many found this type of approach difficult; we were, after all, a group of people who had come together to work not to worship!

Let us imagine a scene other than the one we are in. We are going to be aware from time to time of noises and sounds around us and you may be able to make them part of this imaginary world. I would like you to work hard at filling in the detail in your mind as I paint the general picture. I will leave time for you to do this, and in these pauses you should use your imagination to fill in the scene around you. If you are in a room then look at the floor to see if there's a carpet, look around to see if there is any furniture and if there are any other people in the room. If you are outside then think about what the weather is like, what sounds or smells surround you, whether or not you can see anyone you know, what are you thinking about as you walk along. But remember that you are not trying to be anyone else: you are you, imagining another life. So forget where you are now and travel in your mind to this other place. It is a house in one of the poorer areas of São Paulo, the biggest city in Brazil. It is early morning and you have just woken up. The other members of your family are still all asleep in the same room.

For some reason this morning you notice the heaviness of the hot air, the acrid smell from the nearby chemical works that keeps going even through the night. You feel slightly unwell, but not more so than usual. You get up and dress quickly without waking anyone and go outside.

It is the start of another day. Jobs have been very hard to get recently, even for someone like yourself who is fitter than most and keen to put in a good day's work. As you walk into town the streets are is just coming to life. You look around, saying hello to the people you know.

You see a notice outside the local bottling plant: 'Workers wanted, apply inside'. There are only a few of you around at this time of the morning so you are lucky. 'What is the work?' you ask. Some cleaning, stacking the crates, emptying the washer, and the pay is 50 cruzados for the day. That's very fair money, a good night tonight for the family, a decent meal, and enough for tomorrow as well. Pity about the dozens in your street who will miss the chance.

You begin the job, taking the hot bottles off the line as they come out of the washer and putting them in the crates. The work is steady; time passes.

You look up and who should you see but your neighbour walking in. It must be after nine because it usually takes her till then to help her old mother get up and get settled. She will be pleased to get work. Usually all the casual jobs have gone by the time she can get out. The washer hisses, the bottles keep coming. Who would have thought that people drank so much?

The work may not be too hard but it certainly is tedious. The twelve o'clock break is very welcome. They even have a canteen here, and fifty cents for the stew is money well spent. You feel much better, you must have needed that food. As you finish eating you notice a group of men by the door. Aren't they wearing those clothes that the district penitentiary gives to newly-released prisoners? The owners must be desperate for labour if they'll take on people like that.

Back to work, this time keeping the floor clear of reject caps and corks. As you push the broom you feel a twinge. You hope the backache is nothing serious, there is no way that you can afford to go to the doctors, let alone pay for any treatment.

Mid-afternoon. As you switch back to the bottle-washing machine there is a disturbance. It's two of those people from that home where they keep those who are mentally ill. What on earth can they do? Ah! it's some form of occupational therapy, sorting out the bottle caps from the corks. Well, they seem to be enjoying themselves. You think that they are lucky having some sort of a home; there are too many simple people just living on the streets these days.

Not long to knocking off time now. What's this, has something happened? There at the door is your neighbour's mother. Is she ill, has there been a fire? But no, they are giving her a chair and letting her sort out the labels. OK, if it makes her feel wanted, it's a lot better than being stuck in the house all day. She sees' you and waves. You wave back and give her a smile.

Another forty-five minutes and the hooter goes. What a feeling: the day's over, the work is finished and it's pay-out time. You get in the queue for the cash office holding your clocking-on slip. You look at the people ahead of you. This is the best part of the day and you think about how you will spend your wages.

But what's this? You can't believe it, they are all getting fifty cruzados: that old woman, those lunatics, those criminals. Well, maybe there will be some sort of bonus, you've worked three or four times as long as some of them. But no, you just get fifty. 'Well, we did agree it,' says the owner. 'Don't you want me to be generous to those others?'

You are thinking many things as you walk away from the Vineyard Bottling Company.

Until 1987 we also took a whole day, once a year, to spend time away from work together, usually in the Northumberland countryside. We would invite an outside speaker to lead a day of reflection, discussion and exploration on themes related to our work. This 'retreat' was reluctantly axed the year that we turned in a major financial loss. As it cost £3,500 in direct charges and lost production time the management group could no longer rate it as a high enough priority. Needless to say this cut was seen by some as further evidence of a slide into apostasy.

At department level most sections had weekly meetings to discuss their work priorities and objectives. These meetings would normally be opened with a reading or prayer, although it would not necessarily be specifically Christian in content. Our weekly senior management meeting was similar, although there, and in other areas, I was always conscious that there were those who felt that we should spend more time praying.

164

Prayer was an issue that we found difficult to cope with as a company. The most likely reason why was that I found prayer a struggle and could not easily reach the reservoir of strength, enlightenment or peace that others could. In this area most of all I was conscious of the fact that my leadership of the organization was at best passive and restraining. We had many people who would have been content with an approach to worship and prayer that had been tried and tested, but these approaches were ones that I found wanting. I was not the person to offer something more constructive, so we remained in a rather uncomfortable, exploratory and experimental state.

When David Jenkins visited us I mentioned this issue rather tentatively as a problem needing a solution. 'Not at all,' he said. 'You have to realize that this is something very positive, don't you see, an opportunity to go forward in faith but in an attitude of discovery and learning.' The comment was made as part of a dialogue with the whole staff and someone then asked, 'What happens if an organization begins to lose its direction and moves away from its original purpose? How is it possible to bring it back on the right path?' 'Well,' said the bishop, 'this is something the church has been doing for two thousand years, and people within it have been dragging it back on course. No, the time comes with any organization when you have to make a fresh start, and it's up to the individuals concerned to recognize the time and the new way forward.'

The bishop was not our only visitor. A wide variety of people came to see us and from time to time we asked local politicians and MPs to give their views on trade and development. We also encouraged clergy from churches on Tyneside to find out about our work and to to pass information about the job opportunities we frequently offered to their congregations. One of the interesting features in the company was how much people found out about the diversity in the local churches. On average people spent five hours a week in church activities, compared with forty hours at Traidcraft. The working day was not necessarily full of theological speculation, but practical issues of faith and theoretical points of belief were very much part of the ordinary conversation. Discussion of religious issues was partly stimulated by the diversity of people's beliefs. Were the members of house churches being dominated by authoritarian pastors? How did the Catholics really justify the Pope's continued refusal to countenance artificial birth control? If Methodists were so keen on preaching why were their sermons so dull? Just what did Anglicans believe?

When asked how working at Traidcraft had changed them, the most common answer from the staff was that they had come to respect and understand other Christian viewpoints and in doing so had expanded, deepened and strengthened their own faith. Above all people felt that many of the compartments between the world and 'the spirit', the natural and the supernatural, were breaking down. This had happened against a practical working background of hammering out the company objectives, of debating redundancies or salary cuts, of voting for staff directors and arguing about unionization, job appraisal, working hours, training and job enrichment. In turn this debate led to many people having a greater degree of confidence about themselves, their own abilities and a new insight as to how the bedrock of faith could underpin the most practical issues.

If there was one strand that ran through all these points it was that of change. In some respects Traidcraft was an uncomfortable place to be, for the nature of the work itself demanded new approaches and constant review. The plaque unveiled on opening day at the Team Valley warehouse read, 'Now I am making the whole of creation new.' As a company we were trying to play our part in that work. The quotation came from the Apocalypse, and it is certainly true that the strands of revelation, discovery and prophetic change were common throughout the great tradition of radical Christian action.

Chris Rowland was a parent of one of the children in my daughter's primary-school class; he was also to become one of Britain's leading theologians, with a particular interest in apocalyptic and issues of justice and liberation. We became good friends, and after he was appointed dean of Jesus College, Cambridge, he became one of the Traidcraft trustees. In a recent book he wrote about the radical Christian tradition.

It has protested against those arrangements which have the appearance of order but which in reality have brought about the prosperity and progress of some at the expense of others. The struggle against injustice remains at the heart of those committed to the good news of Jesus Christ and that means the need to embark upon a course of action, however inadequate it may seem, to remedy it.

Traidcraft's rapid growth had been a strain for an organization that was trying to avoid conventional models and translate management techniques to meet objectives that were, to a large extent, altruistic. For us, 'change' meant progressive and continuing adaption to the demands of the 'market', but our market was not only in products but in ideas and the interpretation of Christian theology. As well as needing to keep alert to our performance on quality, delivery and price we had to be aware that we were operating in a period when public perceptions of society, business and government were altering as never before. As I thought through the theoretical approach to the management of change I found that alongside the straightforward business application I could see parallels with the political and religious sphere. Management of change in Traidcraft had involved steering the commercial growth of a new company as well as seeking ways to broaden the experience of staff and customers on development issues and the way that the Christian faith was relevant to both.

Change is necessary, insisted the accumulated wisdom of the management theorists.

Without change all jobs are terminally at risk. Without change customers become disillusioned. Without change capital is at risk and ultimately is destroyed. Without people-changes capital investment is sub-optimal/non-effective.

The manager then asks what prevents change and receives the following answers:

Change is easier to postpone or avoid than implement. Change is emotionally threatening to most people. Staff largely defend the status quo. Managers tend to concentrate on 'things' rather than on people.

The manager also considers the excuses that are offered to avoid the implementation of change and hears the following:

More study is required. We can't afford it. People will never accept it. The real problem is the market/government/management/staff. We looked at that before. It won't work here. We have to negotiate or consult. It will reduce (existing) employment. You're trying to do too much too soon. You don't understand. We don't need it. It's not relevant to my job.

Finally the manager comes to understand that change is the difference between survival and oblivion. If you fail to change people's attitudes then the failure is absolute. However, the ultimate constraint to achieving change is management itself.

I need to acknowledge a debt to Sir Graham Day, currently the chairman of the Rover Group and Cadbury Schweppes for outlining those points during an after-dinner speech. As he spoke I had a strong feeling that what he was saying had a relevance that was personal as well as corporate. I must have expressed this feeling to him very emphatically later in the evening, because he gave me his notes!

I cannot emphasize too strongly that people are the key elements of change. Traidcraft was an organization established very much on a foundation of principles. Although operating in the commercial sphere and using many commercial techniques its motivation was not financial opportunism. By and large Traidcraft attracted staff who were committed to the underlying issues that the company was trying to promote through its work. Although on the one hand it is a great strength to have a highly motivated group of people working together, their commitment makes it necessary to keep them informed and involved. In practice a whole series of elaborate integrating mechanisms developed to deal with this requirement and still there was a general feeling that people were not kept fully informed.

I have wondered since if we were not asking people to take on too much. Not only were we trying to operate a business using up-to-date management techniques, but we were asking the staff to submit those techniques to a critical evaluation from the perspective of a radical Christian theology that was itself in the process of development. But where else can this sort of thing be done and claim to have any value? When it seemed that we had taken on too much, as it often did, I used to reflect that as Christians we should not be afraid of losing. It was better to try to work out the principles to the best of our ability than to compromise. This approach gave the company the aura of an experimental workshop from time to time, and it was not to everyone's taste. On reflection, people were very tolerant.

12

A Parting of Ways

Early in February 1988 I realized that I either had to make a positive decision about leaving or stay on for at least another two years. I re-read the notes that I had written the previous October and still found myself agreeing with them. Five months seemed long enough to provide some sort of assurance that the feeling was more than my old desire for novelty. I talked it over once again at home with Chris. 'If you think it's the right thing then go ahead,' she said, keeping to herself reservations about how we were going to eat.

The next day I asked Brian and Jan if they would like to have a meal with me after work. I felt that I needed to tell them first as they had been my closest colleagues who were in at the beginning. We went to a pizza restaurant and I ordered spaghetti carbonara. When I reached the critical moment of disclosure I genuinely found that I could not speak. It was something that had never happened to me before. They watched me as I struggled with the words, took a gulp of beer and tried again. 'I think its time I left Traidcraft,' I managed to say at last, my eyes filling with tears. But after that it was easier.

The way that I eventually chose to make the break was to drag out the process of telling people over three weeks. To me the most important announcement was at our regular Thursday meeting for all staff on 25 February. There were a few business items from other people: a visit to the Philippines, staff association elections, and news that the board had approved the budget and that we would be having a detailed presentation of it the following week. Then I took the floor and began.

Those of you with long memories or a feeling for dates and anniversaries realize that next year, sometime between June and August, will be the tenth anniversary of Traidcraft. By that time we will have sold over £20 million worth of goods, supported thousands of people through employment and, I hope, have changed the ideas of quite a few people here about the Third World, about our response as Christians, and put down a few markers about alternative business. We have been thinking that this deserves remembering in some special way, and one of the ideas that we have is to produce a book about Traidcraft.

During this time Traidcraft has been pushing into lots of new areas and we have broken a lot of new ground. The way we operate is still unique, although our structure needs pretty, regular overhaul. Our share issue was the first of its type and we are still the only public company of our kind. We are working on new initiatives in alternative banking. We have established strong links with, and have perhaps had some influence on, Christian Aid, CAFOD, Oxfam, Greenpeace and others. During this time we have seen the development agencies become more professional at the task of assisting the poor and we have seen the churches start to acknowledge the extent to which the gospel is for the poor. We ourselves have been influenced by the churches in the Third World as they work out their own living understanding of the gospels. It is all the more ironic then that I don't think that we can say that the general public in Britain understands the problems of injustice and poverty any better. In fact we see an increasing concentration on money, on getting on, on getting nice things. We've seen selfishness turned from being a private vice into a public virtue.

I've been thinking about these things for a couple of

years now and there is something that I would like to do in response. First, I want to write the Traidcraft book, to reflect on those ten years and set down how everything happened and what was special about it. I also think there might be the bones of another book about alternative trading, about development agencies and the response to poverty amidst growing affluence. And finally I want to put together some ideas, perhaps a new approach to these issues of justice that have concerned me for the last twenty years.

Now there is a problem about doing all this, and that is time. If I'm to do this properly I can't fit it around the responsibilities of being Traidcraft's managing director, and it is not fair at the present time to ask Traidcraft to let me have the time or resources. It's not been an easy decision to make, but the logic of what I've been saying has made me tell the board that I think that during the second half of this year I should be handing on my responsibilities as MD.

A lot of details need to be worked out, but all that is in hand. Traidcraft has come through a difficult time recently, but is now very well placed to keep on building and growing and has a good future ahead. Its prosperity is one of the reasons why I can take this step now. I can also take it knowing that we have all worked hard together over the years to establish Traidcraft's ideas and the way we work. Our approach is now a shared thing and shared so widely amongst all of us that it is secure. That doesn't mean that there won't be struggles if we want to hold on to what we think is different and important about Traidcraft but we have arrived at the end of the beginning and we are in good shape to go forward.

I had managed to finish a large mug of strong Nicaraguan coffee before starting, but still felt as if I was going to gum up. After I finished Jan explained that a group had been established by the board to sort out the details of my leaving and the appointment of a new managing director. Philip added a note that Traidcraft's ideals were a lot bigger than any single person (nicely meant) and then there were a few questions from people whom I had primed to lead off. Then nothing. 'Thank you,' I said, and to close the meeting gave a short reading from Hans Kung on the will of God. 'There is a letter that you can pick up on the way out which sets down some of what I said,' I concluded; and that was it. Two days previously the board had scarcely reacted to my announcement, and now the same thing was happening with the rest of the staff. Only one person during the rest of the day raised the matter at all. I wondered why it was that people found it so hard to say anything. I needed to talk about it in much the same way that one needs to talk about a bereavement, but everything carried on as usual. I struggled with a sense of anti-climax for, after all, wasn't this low key reaction just what I would have wished for?

One of the factors that I had not mentioned publicly but that had encouraged me to move on was the increasing amount of time that was being taken up with discussing the effectiveness of the board and the role of the trustees. The confidence of the non-executive members of the board had been badly shaken the previous year when the company had a major loss. Some board members had little business experience and naturally felt somewhat exposed. Those that did have business experience were being extremely cautious. Philip, as finance director, had done an excellent job during the preceding fifteen months in tightening up budgeting procedures and making more secure the underlying financial stability of the company. Although we had turned a £300,000 loss into a small profit within the year it was clear that a sea change had taken place in attitudes at board level and that it was severely affecting morale throughout the company. Caution and pessimism was not my natural style, nor did I feel that it would benefit Traidcraft if it continued to hang like a miasma over our policy discussions.

In these circumstances I had hoped that the trustees, who controlled the voting shares, would take decisive action to rejuvenate the board and reaffirm the direction and style of the company. But here again, although there were trustees with business experience, the weight of an enterprise with 140 direct employees, tens of thousands of individual customers and with some of the best-known charities in the country as contract customers quite reasonably urged a cautious,'wait and see' approach. I began to feel that my own innate optimism and determination to keep exploring new routes towards social justice were counter-productive. Traidcraft had been established so that effective leadership could be exercised whilst a system of checks and balances ensured that individual executive power would not become too great. I had begun by thinking that I needed to do without Traidcraft, without the cocoon of an organization that increasingly was making me concentrate on the mechanics of power rather than the results of radically-applied business techniques. Now, as the date I had set for leaving came closer, I was wondering how to come to terms with a feeling that Traidcraft would carry on quite well once I had gone.

Perhaps the tensions that arose were inevitable and were merely heightened by the financial rough patch. I had always been a person who wanted to take the next step rather than stop, look around, plan the route and proceed after suitable refreshment. I also had problems in applying myself to detailed administrative work for long stretches. I think that this made me a 'start-up' person and Traidcraft had now become established and in some ways was forcing me into a role for which I was not suited.

I was torn between wanting to play some part in Traidcraft's continuing life and feeling that I should clear the decks so I could concentrate on new work in a related area. There were clearly some people on the board who felt that a clean break would be best, that my leaving would provide an opportunity to introduce a certain type of order and perhaps a more conventional structure into the management of a company that needed to settle down. When I became aware of their attitude I had to think seriously about the rightness of my decision to go. I had always been a firm believer in perpetual revolution, uncomfortable as it might be at times. In my heart I doubted

174

whether the distinctive character of the company could be maintained if it lost its probing approach to business practice and method.

That Traidcraft could continue to be a 'success' in terms of providing a service to Third World producers and other charities I did not doubt. The executive management of the company was strong and the loyalty of customers still apparent. But I felt that both these things needed to be sustained by a spirit of adventure, a continued and often unsettling application of the Christian gospel to the daily task of running a business that was seeking to serve the poor. I talked this through with friend who had also recently ceased to be chief executive of a similar-sized company. 'Don't try and hang on to a few bits,' was his advice. 'Once you have left you'll find yourself in a position to see all the weaknesses more clearly yet you will not have any real power, even as a board member, to make the sort of changes you will want.'

So, probably much to everyone's relief, I went quietly. The formal goodbye on my last day was absolutely right. I was hauled out at lunchtime to sit before the assembled staff and made the subject of a 'This is Your Life'. 'Richard Adams,' it began, 'greengrocer, entrepreneur, thinker, drinker, globe-trotter, fair trader, author-to-be, lion tamer, life guard, astronaut, goat herder and all-round good chap: this is a day to forget as long as you live.' There then followed a pageant of scurrilous, slanderous or excruciatingly embarrassing incidents from the past. All the old chestnuts were paraded with colleagues gleefully taking the parts of old girlfriends and 'difficult' former members of staff. Genuine incidents that I had completely forgotten were recalled such as the summer day when executives from an organization called Investors in Industry called to finalize a loan agreement for £300,000. An eyewitness recalled the look of amazement on their faces when I bounded down the stairs to greet them in sandals, shorts and string vest. It was true. The only time in the previous fifteen years that I had ever worn a suit or tie was as a joke on Red Nose Day.

Taking over from a person who has not only been in post for nine years but who also founded the organization would be a daunting task for anyone. As the applications had come in I had scanned them for someone who, above all, would be both sensitive to the ethos and traditions of Traidcraft and who also had a clear, publicly-recognized competence in an area that the company needed to develop. As soon as I saw the application from Paul Johns I felt that we might have the right person.

Paul was qualified in both accountancy and personnel work but his special area was relations with the news media. As a former chairman of the Campaign for Nuclear Disarmament (CND) he had had plenty of experience and, although he came very much from a 'peace' background, he expressed a vision for Traidcraft that was very positive. Fortunately the selection panel thought the same and so I felt more comfortable packing up the contents of my desk drawers in July. I had talked about some of my concerns to Paul at his interview and knew that he was on our wavelength. 'As I see it,' he said, 'we have to sell to people the benefits of buying Traidcraft — not just useful, decorative, value-for-money products but the opportunity to buy into a better, sharing, caring world.'

I had thought about the effect of leaving something that had been a large part of my life for nine years, but could not predict my reaction. Starting to write this book helped a lot as I set in order the events of the early years. Without writing it all down I think the break would have been more traumatic than it turned out to be. But something else helped as well.

The day before I told the board that I wished to leave I had received a letter entitled 'Towards an Organisation of Creative Consumers'. It came from Paul Ekins, someone whom I knew only distantly as the research director for the Right Livelihood Award, sometimes known as the Alternative Nobel Prize. Paul had also been the first general secretary of the Green Party and had played a big part in establishing the New Economics Foundation, of which I had just become a supporter.

I read the paper he had enclosed and felt that I had to ring him right away. 'Are you saying,' I asked Paul, 'that you think ordinary consumers can change the world if they can be shown how their spending can really make a difference?' 'Yes,' he replied, 'but the message needs to be practical and direct. I want to see the theory put into practice.' 'This is quite a coincidence,' I said. 'I've been groping towards some new, broader vision for the ordinary consumer and I'm just about to tell Traidcraft that I want to leave to spend more time thinking about it.'

Ten weeks later about twenty people met in London to take the idea forward, and as I write, ten months on, the idea seems to be turning into some sort of reality. Maybe it will deserve another book in ten years' time, but in early 1989 I find myself the first director of New Consumer, at the beginning of another organization and just setting out its plan of action.

New Consumer looks forward to an economy based on service and cooperation, a clean and healthy environment, an international market-place that shares, nurtures and sustains the planet's people and resources: a more humane and just economic order. The proposal is that this aim can be achieved by the ordinary consumer. In 1988, £280 billion was spent by individuals in Britain, £1.8 billion was given to charity. New Consumer will inform, mobilize, organize and provide the choices of services and products through which a just and sustainable economy may be built. It will become a key element in directing everyday spending for social progress.

New Consumer will also support and encourage those companies that are moving towards active corporate social responsibility programmes. By informing the consumers it will encourage their vast and influential purchasing power to be used to create a better world.

Thus runs the outline manifesto, and time will tell whether the programme can be made into some sort of reality. As the New Consumer research team assembled in February 1989 I could sense that we all felt that we were starting something far-reaching. The occasion recalled for me the early days of Tearcraft and Traidcraft, but maybe this was because, by another strange coincidence, the offices in Elswick were only three hundred yards from the Skinner's old house where, in 1975, Tearcraft had started.

While I was getting excited about New Consumer, things at Traidcraft were really buzzing. Early in 1988 we had been approached by a number of charities who had previously had their own Christmas catalogues done by other companies and who were looking for a change. Perhaps our good record with Greenpeace had got around, but before I left we had clinched five contracts with other organizations to supply a mail-order merchandise service, and in most cases the deal involved our taking charge of all the product selection, catalogue design and production.

The best time to send out a Christmas catalogue is in early September; as the peak period for sales is the first two weeks of November it is useful to spread the load by encouraging orders early in the season. Unfortunately September 1988 saw the whole of Britain hit by a postal strike. Not only was the dispatch of tens of thousands of catalogues delayed, but thousands of people decided not to order because their pillar boxes were sealed up. Temporary staff taken on at the end of August had to be laid off for a short while until the orders came in with a rush in October. Just as the flow was reaching a peak the main computer crashed. On top of that the picking and packing system was being overwhelmed by the large number of small orders that the new contracts had generated.

I was calling in two or three times a week during November and noticed how the nights and weekends of overtime were taking their toll on staff. Standby computer hardware and sixty temporary staff managed to keep orders flowing, and so by Christmas a record level of business had been done. Paul Johns, the new managing director, had been in post for about four months when, in January 1989, we had a meal together. In many respects it had been a baptism of fire for him but he was thriving on the challenges. 'What I really appreciate,' he said, 'after working as a consultant for so long, is being part of a team in every sense and having a really supportive group of colleagues.'

Naturally I was curious about how Paul saw the company with which I had been so closely involved. 'It's a lot more complex than I thought at first. Sourcing, importing, selling and distributing have so many facets, and when you add to that the distinctive qualities that are special to Traidcraft you have a very sophisticated operation. We impose limitations on ourselves because of the way we buy and who we buy from and this doesn't make things easier in commercial terms. But how do we judge Traidcraft's success? Surely not by its commercial viability? For me being profitable is a condition of operating, not the be all and end all.'

Paul went on to say that one of the criteria he would use in judging the company's success was the impact that it was having on public opinion, even on public policy. 'One of the the reasons that I joined Traidcraft and believe in it is that I see it as a campaigning as well as a commercial organization.' Paul's experience with the CND had given him extensive knowledge of how powerful and successful public campaigns could be mounted. 'Ordinary individuals are very limited in what they can do and we have to recognize that. However, great changes can occur in the world when you get a buildup of public opinion as a result of campaigning for many many years, and it eventually coincides with some critical event or initiative taken by a major politician. I think it is perfectly reasonable to assume that Traidcraft can be a major influence in this way, a catalyst in making justice in trade a major issue.

'The Christian community may be our core market,' he went on, 'but there are lots of people who aren't Christians, who don't want to join campaigns or organizations, but who are concerned about world poverty and threats to the environment on which all of us, rich and poor alike, depend.' Coming from 'outside' Paul was perhaps more able to make a realistic assessment of Traidcraft's public visibility than those of us who had been wrapped up in it for nearly a decade. 'It's nothing like as well-known as I think it should be,' he said. 'And this is perhaps encouraging as it means there are plenty of people out there who can become our customers. My priority for the coming months is definitely sales promotion. The products aren't as accessible as they should be: we need more mail-order customers, more reps and more sales through ordinary shops. In particular the products have to be presented at the point of sale more attractively than they are at the moment.'

As part of the recovery plan put forward in 1987 we had agreed to operate a slightly more conventional sales approach on the main range. The policy of making the main mail-order catalogue sell the products rather than the ideas had paid off. Mail-order business for Traidcraft products was up by more than 25 per cent. The catalogue was very different from those of previous years having only 7 per cent of its space devoted to background information about producers or the underlying ideas concerning trade and development. Five years earlier we had taken a very different line with nearly 30 per cent of the catalogue giving details about the producing groups and how Traidcraft was seeking to develop an alternative business style.

In contrast the amount of material being produced for reps to use had dramatically increased. An educational materials catalogue now contained over a hundred items, and specialist staff were designing shop and exhibition displays and developing a programme for schools. But this had taken place against a movement towards a more 'professional' selling approach for the products. At the end of 1988 the board confirmed this strategy by deciding to appoint a sales director. The fact that Traidcraft had taken ten years to make such an appointment might just have reflected a subconscious feeling that the products on offer should sell themselves. After all, if people only understood the background about where the goods came from and how much their sale could help the poor then surely they would buy them? I heartily agreed with Paul Johns as he summed up his philosophy for promoting Traidcraft for the future. 'We have a message as well as products to sell. Good ideas aren't self-evident any more than good products. Whether we like it or not we've got to be prepared to push what we have to say as well as what we have to sell. We owe it to our producers to do so.'

13

A Sense of Direction

Ten years on is as good a time as any to look back and evaluate. Thousands of people have each spent thousands of hours of their lives working with or for Traidcraft. Has it been time well spent? Traidcraft puts the service of others first, so it is important to know if the millions of hours devoted to its activities have been put at the service of the poor and disadvantaged more effectively.

Previously I set out the objectives by which Traidcraft decided to measure itself, but self assessment has its problems. However, using conventional commercial indicators, particularly those relating to financial success, would not bring out those areas of innovation and achievement of which the company is most proud. In trying to make some comment on the work of Traidcraft after ten years I would therefore like to use some of the insights that are being developed by business people who are coming together in many countries to share their desire for a better world.

These ideas have been given a voice through the international forum of the Other Economic Summit; through bodies such as the International Organisation of Consumer Unions or the Grameen Bank in Bangladesh; through groupings of business people in the Social Venture Network in the United States and the Business Network in Britain; through the practical mass movement of 500,000 ordinary consumers in the Seikatsu Club in Japan. Traidcraft is a contemporary of all these groups and like all of them recognizes that we have lost the balance between economic achievement and personal and social development. Traidcraft draws strongly on the Christian tradition and experience and recognizes the need for spiritual growth and integration in business. Others draw on different spiritual or philosophical traditions, and what is emerging is a broadly based view of what a 'holistic' business should be doing.

Christians have not been the only people to put words together in such a way as to weave them into a fence around their beliefs, and the jargon that has developed is extensive. Nevertheless, I will try not to use words and phrases such as holistic, networking, transformation, open space, planetary change, experiential, or inner being in defining this new approach to business. I think that it is possible to use plain English to set out a model of the way that any organization, commercial, voluntary, or governmental, should be reacting to our world of expanding ideas, accelerating change and bitter fragmentation.

Recognizing the value of staff. First of all we need to look at the people who make the business function: the staff who work together on a daily basis. A key question to ask is whether they understand and identify with the overall aims of their business. We should be looking for evidence of a breaking-down of barriers between work and the rest of life and an increase in workplace opportunities for personal development.

A long-running slogan of Traidcraft's is 'people before profit', and certainly this has always been meant to include staff as well as producers and customers. In 1985 and 1986 the company drew on the key ideas of a few individuals to involve all staff in setting out the company objectives. It also committed itself to a regular review involving staff, shareholders, customers and producing groups every two years. Although this review did not take place in 1988 due to pressure of work, it remains very much on the agenda.

There is, however, a feeling that less time is spent in working through fundamental issues such as the causes of poverty, the role of our consumer society in perpetuating divisions between rich and poor, how Christians should respond and how they should work with others. When the company came under financial pressures in 1987 it was calculated that an hour-long educational or discussion meeting of all the staff cost nearly £500. In addition there was the growing problem of finding 'something for everyone'. This was one of the problems of size: how to make more than 130 people feel that they were working as a team. When morale needs to be high, such as peak periods or times of financial stress, there is great pressure to meet targets and perhaps less time for stepping back and seeing the overall picture.

In spite of this a visitor to Traidcraft certainly notices something special. Some months after I had left I had the opportunity to take someone round the operation who was in the process of expanding an existing commercial mail-order business. She phoned me up the next day. 'I spent all my time going back on the train to London thinking and planning,' she told me. 'I walked into my bosses' office this morning and said, "We've just got to work with those people." I can't tell you how impressed I was with the people I met. They were so open, friendly and helpful. I thought, "This is the way business should be done."'

Making things happen. It is vital for a company not only to have good ideas but to make sure that they are put into practice. In any company, there is always pressure to make economies, but it is vital that important areas of development are not neglected.

Traidcraft has been through a period of development where it has expanded into the available space and then, just as the walls seemed about to crack, found another floor, or another building. In 1985 plans were laid to expand yet again into a second new warehouse. Although these plans were postponed for good reasons, the consequences of inaction were really showing up by the end of 1988. People are influenced by their working conditions, and it was generally agreed that these were only just about tolerable at the beginning of 1989. Again, financial constraints had meant belt-tightening, but many people were wondering if this policy was going to be counter-productive.

Traidcraft consistently promoted people from within, and of the permanent staff employed at the end of 1988 nearly 70 per cent had moved up from their original jobs. But some of the surrounding personnel policies were beginning to creak a little. The training budget had not increased with staff size, the job evaluation scheme needed a major overhaul and job appraisal had effectively ground to a halt after only one year of operation. In all cases there were explanations relating to time and money but people were getting the message that staff development was less important then the bottom line. I think that it is important to recognize that this sort of pressure existed and that even a company with a strong 'culture' and the day-by-day, week-by-week mechanisms of sharing and discussing was affected.

It is particularly important for executives to ensure that people get clear and decisive management. Occasionally this will involve making some criticism; more often it will mean giving praise, but in all circumstances it will mean providing constructive support. Once again, it is hardest to do so when the company is under pressure, and certainly it was something that I know all the senior executives needed when we were coping with a major loss and the subsequent period of retrenchment from early 1987. We formed our own self-support group and tried to give each other pats on the back as we passed each milestone on the road to recovery.

But Traidcraft survived this rough patch and continues to push ahead. It is an organization which, after ten years, is clearly still going places. It still has within it the ability to apply resources to ideas that are innovative, alternative, even 'prophetic'. As I write Traidcraft is playing a leading role in seeking to establish an international 'Tradebank', it is working for a close federation of nine alternative trading organizations in Europe and is chairing a worldwide association of ATOs that aims to give a real voice to the disadvantaged in the area of international trade.

I believe that the radical approach that Traidcraft has been trying to develop and practise is still desperately needed within the church as a whole as well as within the business community generally and the 'alternative' movement in particular. For the role of Traidcraft is not to demonstrate another successful aspect of the enterprise culture; primarily Traidcraft enables people who believe that love and justice should be articulated in trade to demonstrate their concern. Its role is linked with an increasing discussion in the churches concerning the nature of the Christian response to poverty and injustice.

At the end of 1988 it seemed that Traidcraft had played a significant part in widening this discussion, but clearly the average person in Britain was not deeply interested in the complexities of development theory. Nevertheless, there are live and very important issues on which more people need to hold an informed opinion. People need to know what is the rationale for supporting Christian initiatives to help the poor, especially the desperately poor in the developing world, through agencies such as TEAR Fund, Christian Aid, CAFOD, and World Vision. That short list is significant. Those four organizations handle over 85 per cent of the £55 million donated in the UK to relief and development through non-missionary yet specifically Christian channels. By contrast there are more than 150 UK missionary societies with approximately the same overall income. The top ten societies receive about 30 per cent of the total donated.

In what way has the Christian response to poverty in the Third World changed since 1945? At that point none of the Christian development agencies existed. Nine of the top ten missionary organizations were founded in the eighteenth or nineteenth centuries, and 80 per cent of the total were more than fifty years old. What distinguishes the Christian relief and development organizations from the missionary societies and why were they established? To what extent has the role of the missionary organization changed since the establishment of the development agencies?

In some respects Traidcraft has ploughed a very narrow furrow by confining its work to justice in trade. As a result it has not been asked many of the questions that can be levelled at the Christian development agencies. How do they differ from each other? What do they see as their objectives and priorities? How are their policies affected by the views of donors? Can they be affected by the views of aid recipients? What criteria are used for selecting partners and projects? What approach do they take to educating supporters? What degree of cooperation exists between each of them and between them and other non-Christian agencies? How do they see the future regarding Christian development work?

These are all important issues, not least because the churches and their congregations contribute proportionally more to development assistance and relief than the rest of the population. Almost by accident Traidcraft has made the possibility of having a constructive debate on these questions more likely. By putting the emphasis on trade in its own work it has broadened the whole development debate. There is perhaps a long way to go before public opinion on trade and justice issues shifts sufficiently to make politicians change direction, but a start has been made.

Acting on behalf of others. This story has been written from a First World viewpoint and will mainly be read by those who are wealthy beyond the dreams of the average Traidcraft supplier. Traidcraft's work depends on offering an alternative approach whereby the rich can recognize and respond to the needs of the poor. The structures and the systems must be different, but the finest 'people sensitive' organization counts for nothing unless it genuinely is setting out a way for the vast majority of the world, who cluster around the margins of our affluence, to be drawn in. So far this has not happened. It is true that many thousands of people in the Third World have directly benefitted through Traidcraft, but for each one that has there have been a thousand asking, 'What about me?'

This is the point at which this record of Traidcraft's history comes to an end. Traidcraft, of course, continues. Each year that passes will mean that a new chapter could be written. That the scale of the work sometimes seems like a drop in the ocean is irrelevant. We must all have reflected about our own place as an individual in a world of five billion. Yet we know that in every generation there are people who can change the course of history. The same is true of organizations.

I believe that in its efforts to change the world Traidcraft is digging in for the long haul. In 1968, when I first began to think about the issues touched on in the preceding chapters, there was a tangible sense of optimism in the air. Economic growth, technology and goodwill were surely capable of making a real impact on the world's problems. The following twenty years brought some hope but mostly disillusion. But now a new spirit is once again stirring. We will not get a new heaven and a new earth overnight, but we do not need to despair and we must keep trying. As people we have shown an amazing capacity for change. There is just a hint that we might also be finding a sense of direction.

Some Facts and Figures Supplied
by Traidcraft plc

1. SALES PATTERN AND GROWTH

1.1 The accompanying chart and table show how sales have grown and what the mix of sales is.

1.2 The company sells to:

direct mail-order customers	34%
customers via voluntary representatives	48%
trade customers and agents	15%
others	3%
	100%

2. EMPLOYMENT IN THE UK

Traidcraft employs about 150 people (some part-time) in its main premises at Gateshead, in its shops and regional offices.

3. EMPLOYMENT IN THE THIRD WORLD

3.1 In pursuit of justice in trade, Traidcraft aims to provide work and economic benefits for families of the world's poorest countries, by offering an outlet in the Uk for their skills and goods.

3.2 The more the value added to the product in the country of origin, the better for the people who live there. The company encourages local producers to process and pack their products wherever possible.

3.3 With sales of goods from Third World sources expected to exceed £3 million in 1990, Traidcraft's orders to its overseas partners probably represent sufficient income to sustain more than 4,000 families for a year.

4. TRAIDCRAFT'S DEVELOPMENT AND EDUCATIONAL WORK

4.1 In addition to the direct benefit from sales which goes to our producers and suppliers, a percentage of our sales (more that £50,000 per annum, particularly Christmas cards) goes to, for example, Christian Aid, CAFOD. The company also help to fund the work of Traidcraft Exchange — its associated charitable trust.

4.2 The 'Development Unit' of Traidcraft Exchange is a growing service of consultancy and technical assistance to producer groups (who may or may not be Traidcraft suppliers).

4.3 Traidcraft Exchange also helps to increase public awareness of development issues associated with trade by providing the company with educational information and material which is an integral part of its sales.

5. TRAIDCRAFT'S SHAREHOLDERS

Traidcraft has £1,375,151 of issued share capital divided into three classes of shares.

5.1 Voting Shares (£50,150) of which 96.3% are owned by the Traidcraft Exchange, our parent charity. The Trustees of the Exchange, through their power to appoint Directors of the Company, fulfil a duty under the Deed of Mutual Covenant to uphold the Foundation Principles of Traidcraft as a company committed to bringing love and justice into international trade.

5.2 Non-Voting Shares (£1,325,000), raised through two successful share issues in 1984 and 1986, providing the core financing of the company's growth. These shares are held by some 3,000 shareholders, mostly private individuals.

These shares can be bought and sold. Details of how to become a shareholder can be obtained from the Assistant Company Secretary, Traidcraft plc, Kingsway, Gateshead NE11 0NE.

5.3 Guardians' Share (£1) There is one Guardians' Share owned by Tradefair Guardians' Share Company Limited which exists solely to prevent control of Traidcraft falling into the hands of a person or persons who might seek to change its trading principles.

6. REPRESENTING TRAIDCRAFT

6.1 Much of Traidcraft's success over the past ten years can be put down to voluntary representatives. Currently they account for about half the company's sales, and their work in promoting Traidcraft has provided the company with a secure base on which to build.

6.2 The 'Reps Scheme' provides scope for increased involvement in the Traidcraft vision. As well as supplying friends and contacts with Traidcraft goods, reps gain opportunities locally to raise awareness about issues of justice and development. The company assists them by providing credit terms, discount and special offers, and a regular free newsletter and cassette-tape which keeps them up-to-date on the news and issues.

6.3 An information pack with full details about how to become a rep is available from Traidcraft, Kingsway, Gateshead, NE11 0NE (Tel. 091 491 0591).

Traidcraft Sales

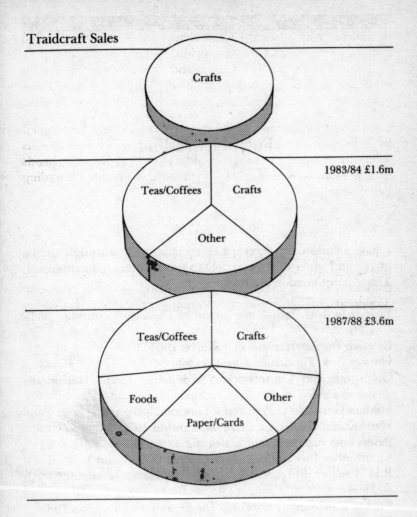

1983/84 £1.6m

1987/88 £3.6m

	1979/80	1983/84	1987/88	1988/89 (estimated)
Third World goods	100,000	1,400,000	2,650,000	2,800,000
Other		200,000	950,000	1,300,000
Total sales	100,000	1,600,000	3,600,000	4,100,000

Further Reading

I have occasionally referred to specific books throughout the book and I also owe a great debt to many others not mentioned. Those mentioned in the text are:

Leonardo Boff, *Introducing Liberation Theology*, Tunbridge Wells 1987

Dietrich Bonhoeffer, *Ethics*, London 1964

Harvey Cox, *The Secular City*, London 1965

Goldsmith and Clutterbuck, *The Winning Streak*, Harmondsworth 1985

Mikhail Gorbachev, *Perestroika*, London 1987

Hans Kung, *On Being a Christian*, London 1976

Peters and Waterman, *In Search of Excellence*, New York 1982

Christopher Rowlands, *Radical Christianity*, London 1988

R.H. Tawney, *Religion and the Rise of Capitalism*, Harmondsworth 1964

Robert Townsend, *Further Up The Organisation*, London 1985

Max Weber, *The Protestant Ethic and the Spirit of Capitalism*, London 1952

I would also recommend *Comfortable Compassion*, Charles Elliott, London 1987, and *Understanding Organisations*, Charles Handy, Harmondsworth 1981. Both offer penetrating analyses on some of the issues touched on in this book.